THE WINDOW

A true story

By

Gregory Lloyd-Wadsworth

This book is dedicated to our mother Flo who endured the unendurable and to my brother Ken who saved her.

CONTENTS

CHAPTER 1	CAROLINA	4
CHAPTER 2	LITTLE RED	10
CHAPTER 3	BONES	17
CHAPTER 4	THE BRIDES OF CHRIST	27
CHAPTER 5	THE LUNATIC ASYLUM	41
CHAPTER 6	MY SALVATION BEGINS	51
CHAPTER 7	BLUE BIRDS AND CORN FLOWERS	55
CHAPTER 8	MOMMY, WHAT'S A PERVERT?	60
CHAPTER 9	GOD, I NEED A CIGARETTE!	63
CHAPTER 10	THE LUNATICS ARE IN CHARGE	66
CHAPTER 11	THE OSCAR GOES TO…	68
CHAPTER 12	FREEDOM	71
CHAPTER 13	WHOS YOUR DADDY?	76
CHAPTER 14	GOING SOMEWHERE?	83
CHAPTER 15	DINNER TIME	87
CHAPTER 16	BARNETT WAY	92
CHAPTER 17	RUN HONEY! RUN!	100
CHAPTER 18	THE WINDOW	112
CHAPTER 19	HAPPY BIRTHDAY SON	126
CHAPTER 20	ESCAPE TO OZ	131
CHAPTER 21	POST-MORTEM	137

PROLOGUE

Much of this book was written from what I remember as a child, and at times from a child's perspective. To protect the innocent, I have changed some family names, the street name and the house number where this house still stands to this day.

God only knows what goes on in that house now.

Each one of us on this insignificant planet have secrets of some kind which, for many reasons, remain hidden and locked away deep inside of us. Secrets we choose to keep buried whether we want to or not. Some of us may choose to ignore them and others, like myself, try all our lives coming to terms with the hand that was dealt to us when growing up. My life has been spent trying to forget and forgive or at best exorcise my hidden demons so that I can try to live a normal life. Who knows if its better this way, maybe not, time will tell?

This book has taken me the better part of fifty-five years of my life to write and it's time to move on. Enough is enough. However, in trying to do so, my thoughts and memories came back to me in torrents of emotion where it all overwhelmed me to the point of giving up. I pick my pages up, look at it, play with the pages and try and write a few lines down before it becomes once again too much. Then the demons, night terrors and horrors of my childhood come back for me. They love to taunt and play with me as they drag me slowly back into their world.

As they will again when I sleep tonight.

The familiar signs of sadness and despair sweep over me, it's then time for me to lay it down, put it away for another day, another time. I have been told by various people throughout my life, some professional and others who just enjoy giving their two cents worth of advice, that it will, "All will get better as you get older," "Try putting it all behind you," "Ignore it" or bluntly, "Move on!" What fools they all are. Everybody means well of course, but for me my safety mechanism is to pretend it never happened. Unfortunately, reality doesn't work like that.

The old saying, "Out of sight out of mind" has never worked for me, as simple everyday things can set off a memory and it all comes back, dragging me once again into the depths of despair. Sometimes certain smells, colours or what people say will unexpectedly trigger it for me. So, I continually stumble through life, trying the best I can to cope daily to string a type of normal existence together to show everybody and myself that I am okay. In doing so I'm able to mask my past so I can pretend that everything is indeed completely normal.

With the ongoing pretence and fake smiles came the lying. Mom and I were always reinventing ourselves trying to project normality to everyone. Especially to 'him.' We would do anything to hide the truth of our everyday existence. I became very good at it. Mom and I had exhausted the better part of our lives in this futile attempt to make life look as normal as possible to the other people that lived near us. However, the neighbours who lived on Barnett Way who made it their business to know our business, knew differently.

No one would ever dare to interfere if they knew what was good for them. To them, we were the horror freak show you were too scared to watch but could never turn away from, yet never get involved. I could always see the neighbours sneaking a peek through their curtains looking at the next instalment of this never-ending show coming from our house. Sometimes you would see their doors slightly ajar so they wouldn't miss the screams, foul swear words along with the crashing sounds of things being destroyed.

Mom tried so hard to project normality to anyone who would be remotely interested in us and to show them that we were just like they were - happy, well-adjusted, hard-working people. When we did meet anyone in the street, we got a nervous smile or a quick nod as they hurried passed us. The healthier option, for them, was to keep well away from us, as many did. Sometimes Mom and I would see what we thought was a friendly neighbour coming our way only to see them quickly cross the street to get away so they wouldn't have to make polite conversation with us. We tried hard to look and be like everyone else who lived in Barnett Way, but it never worked out. It was painfully obvious we were an embarrassment to the entire neighbourhood. That's what it's all about isn't it? Trying to look and act like everyone expects you to be all the time. Whether we like it or not, we are constantly being judged and scrutinized, sometimes by the very people we don't even know. We tried so hard to ensure that no one must know, no one must find out our dirty little secrets, and what went on in the House on Barnett Way.

Here is my story about my mother's choices and the impact they had on all our lives.

Revenge is futile if you are powerless to follow through with it.

Chapter 1

CAROLINA

I suppose if this story has a beginning it starts with my maternal Grandmother whose name was Carolina.

'Grandma' was born on December 3, 1880 and came from a village in the south eastern part of Switzerland named Lodrino, close to the country that was called 'The Kingdom of Italy.' Carolina never learned to speak English but was fluent in spoken and written High German (Hochdeutsch), Italian, French and Austrian (lingua franca; Austro-Bavarian).

She married a brutish and lazy man by the name of Enrico (Henry), who was born on December 7, 1875 in a small town called Novara, in the Piedmont region in the northwest of present-day Italy (I say present-day as back in the 19th and early 20th century's cities and towns were constantly being swallowed up by major powers of the day for territorial gain). She would often say, "I would go to sleep at night and wake up to find out that the country I had gone to bed in, was now part of another country."

Her duties in life were plain and simple - obey, work and bear children to work her husband's farm. She did this without question throughout her wretched life. Life was miserable with her large brood of eleven children and they existed in abject poverty. No-one really knows exactly where her eleven children were born because boundaries and borders were constantly shifting as fast as families did in pre-World War I Europe.

In the early part of the twentieth century the mainstream of European immigration departed for America from Southampton, England or Ireland and various ports of Europe. It was at this time Grandpa Enrico decided to leave Italy leaving

Carolina and the children behind. He sailed to America from Southampton on an American ship called the *St Paul*, arriving in New York City on June 5, 1904. By train he finally made his way to northern California and decided to settle in the region of present-day Humboldt County. He rented a ramshackle farm of twenty acres not far from the town of Alton with the dream of getting rich quick.

My Grandmother, Carolina, followed six years later. The long separation was due to the lack of money as all of Grandfather's get rich schemes never panned out. Finally, at the age of thirty, she was able to pack their meagre belongings and with her eleven children set off from their home in northern Italy in late 1910 for the "new world" called America.

The weather conditions at the time were atrocious with a freezing winter throughout Europe in late 1910 and early 1911.

She travelled most of time on foot, hitching lifts whenever possible and begging for rides on any horse and cart that might be going their way. Food was scarce and when they had used up most of their meagre supplies, they begged for it and at times stole from farmers' fields digging up potatoes at night as they slowly moved on towards their departure port.

Grandma, knowing the tensions that had been simmering off and on throughout Europe, consciously avoided the countries and territories belonging to either the Austro-Hungarian or the Prussian (Preussen) Empire/German Empire of Europe. Instead she crossed through the centre of Switzerland and slowly progressed towards the northern part France. On she pressed through various cities, towns and villages many of which would later be destroyed in the up and coming "Great War" (WW1), that began July 28,1914. They finally reached the end of their journey at the port city of Le Havre, France.

Grandma was originally scheduled to sail out from Bremerhaven, in northern Germany. Due to ongoing tensions between the great powers of Europe she decided to now leave through the port town of Le Havre, Normandy, a northern port of France on the Atlantic coast. At the time, it was the second largest port in France after Marseille. From here, they were to set sail for New York on the French steam ship *La Bretagne*. The *La Bretagne* was a French owned and built ship which was steamed driven with a top speed of 17 knots (31 km/h). When launched, she was to carry 390 passengers in first, 65 in second and 600 in third class. However, by launch date of September 9, 1896, third class was tripled from 600 to 1,500 passengers. Throughout her long career, *La Bretagne* was christened a 'jinx' ship. On one cruise a drunken father threw his 5-year-old son overboard and was immediately put into a strait jacket. Cholera and dysentery made their way regularly through the cramped lower decks throughout her many crossings of the Atlantic. Pilot error once resulted in the *La Bretagne* ploughing through a pier, ripping a 49-foot (15metre) hole through the pier causing 11 bulkhead plates in the ship to be crushed. On another occasion, a ship called the *Barbarossa* rammed the starboard side of *La Bretagne* inflicting a 25-foot (7.6metre) hole below her water line. In 1923 her name was changed to the *Alesia*, but she was soon towed away for scrap only to break loose running aground on the island of Texel, northern Holland. *La Bretagne* was now lost.

On arrival at Le Havre docks my Grandmother was told there was no cabin available to accommodate her large family. She was given the options of waiting for a larger Cunard ship or to stay on the *La Bretagne* and bunk down, with all the children, under a tarpaulin on an open deck. The Cunard ship was ruled out due to the cost and time pressures and so she chose the latter, travelling huddled all together for the long crossing of the Atlantic Ocean. The large family joined another 1,055 passengers, now bound for a new life in a country called America.

There was no-one willing to help her as she was just one woman, amongst hundreds of others on board this overcrowded, heaving mass of humanity. She wanted desperately to turn back and go home to a place she knew and felt safe. No-one understood her, no-one seemed to care.

Two of her beloved children died during the voyage from cholera and were hurriedly, and with little ceremony, buried at sea. Grandma would tearfully remember that day was not so much a burial but that her two children were "literally dumped overboard like garbage." By now Grandma was desolate and grief-stricken. To this day I cannot imagine what hardship she must have endured in this massive undertaking to get to a strange and far away country. She was still alone and caring for her nine remaining children and not able to speak this language called English.

After eight long days and seven long nights, the nightmare crossing was coming to an end. At long last, they viewed the Statue of Liberty emerging from the dense New York morning fog. Slowly they trudged through the immigration lines of Ellis Island with all the other people that were being emptied out of Europe's towns and cities. The customs officers simply stamped, 'From Italy' on her papers. That apparently covered all their bases for the family's entry to the United States. They were in awe as they had never seen the likes of a city such as New York.

They arrived exhausted and frightened on a bitterly cold, February 28, 1911.

The struggle continued for Carolina, as she and her nine children made their way across the USA by passenger trains when they could afford it and at other times by begging for a lift on freight trains that hopefully was going west. Eventually reuniting with her husband, Enrico at his farm in Alton, Northern California. Another major hurdle she faced was adopting to the new language. Her ignorance of English left her feeling isolated from the general community. This sense was exaggerated by the fact that few other adults on adjacent farms chose to speak English. Instead they persisted with their native languages of Danish or Portuguese and of course, Swiss Italian only in her family home. She began to think it was a terrible mistake leaving home in the first place as it seemed they were no better off.

It must have seemed to my grandmother that her "new" life was very similar to what she had left behind in Italy - a never-ending battle finding money to feed and clothe her ever growing family. Grandfather's solution was to send most of the children, regardless of age, to work in the nearby towns or farm fields. Anything they could do would help bring money and food into the house. An example of the chronic poverty was the fact that they (the children) never owned a pair of shoes. Everyone walked barefoot to church, school or town whatever the season or weather. Since everyone else was in the same predicament no-one felt ashamed. If the older kids ever had a pair of shoes, they were jealously guarded and, when the day came that they could no longer fit into them, they were reluctantly handed down to the next in line. It didn't matter if you were a male or female. You wore what was given to you and one size did fit all. If the shoes were too big for the "new" owner, they would be stuffed with straw or old newspapers. When the time came for Mom to own her much coveted pair of shoes she didn't care if they were once her brother's or that her toes were now sticking out from the frayed stitching. Stuffing in newspaper soon remedied the fact that they were too big. None of that mattered as she, at last, had her own pair of shoes. It was her Holy Grail Moment and they were just as good as any new pair.

Cinderella couldn't have been happier.

As is typical for many Italians, food, or to be more precise, lack of it was my Grandmother's over-riding concern. She came up with a rotational system where half of her children would be allowed to eat one night, and the other half would go to bed without anything to eat. Everyone ate, but only every other night.

Necessity is truly the mother of all inventions.

A good meal always consisted of boiled potatoes in a broth soup with any remaining potato peelings or vegetables and stale bread thrown into it to bulk it up. A bad one meant you went to bed without anything as it was your turn to go without.

Although on Grandpa's immigration papers he stated he was a farmer, he in fact knew very little about the farming process as all the work was left up to his wife and children. My mother often said he was a "lazy no good bastard and only liked fucking, drinking and laying about half naked in his underpants while his wife and kids slaved, their backs hunched over his fields all day and night digging up potatoes."

Altogether, Carolina gave birth to another 5 children in California. Counting her and Enrico she now had 16 mouths to feed and to worry about.

Such was my Grandmother's new life in sunny California, literally barefoot and constantly pregnant where she finally passed away, alone in her tiny one room shack in 1965. She was 85.

Chapter 2

LITTLE RED

After many miscarriages Carolina managed to at long last carry a child to full term, my mother was born on March 23, 1918 and was named after the beautiful city of Firenze the northern part of Italy grandma remembered and loved so well. On her birth certificate her name was angelized to Florence and shortened by her friends to Flo. Years later she became known as 'Little Red' or just 'Red' to her close friends. She was the first American born to Carolina and Enrico – and was soon followed by several more siblings.

Mom was only able to go to year 6 in school as she was forced to leave by her father, at the age of twelve, to find work and make money for her needy family. Food was the all abiding necessity and was forever in short supply. Although she was quite gifted in maths and had won several awards at her school, her father thought it was a complete waste of time for any girl to be good at anything other than making babies, working and looking after a man - preferably him. To my mother it seemed, work and money were more important for keeping food on the table and to placate her ever-demanding father. One day, she was pulled from school by her father and sent out to find work in the fields or town to do anything that earned the family some money.

Mom would often say that she loved school more than anything in the world, but that hunger and responsibility were quite another thing. At twelve years of age her first job was in a Chinese laundry, as a laundress, working 12-hour days. The money she earned not only helped with the short falls of food but kept her younger siblings in school longer than she could ever have hoped for herself. She would daydream of a better life someday and wanted more from it than the endless drudgery of washing other people's dirty clothes for the meagre pay she received. So, when she turned a respectable age of eighteen in 1936, she shocked her family by packing her bags and left the farm life well and truly behind her. Some of her siblings to this day have resented her for doing this to them as it suddenly stopped the flow of money coming into the house, causing them to quit school and go to work as Mom had done before. She thought it was high time for all of them to grow up and know that there was a life outside the farm and digging for potatoes and that Mom wouldn't be around anymore to support them or her lazy good-for-nothing father.

Grandpa called her a 'Puttana' (Italian for whore) as she walked out the door. Mom fired back with "Il tuo" or roughly translated means "Up yours"!

Mom was eighteen when war clouds were beginning to make their first rumblings across Europe in 1936. Most Americans had little knowledge or interest of the political events in Europe. From their perspective it was, something for the Europeans to figure out, not for the Americans to once again get involved in a European war. As the years slowly went by Mom went from factory to factory. Work was work and she was determined never to go hungry ever again. And then one day in 1941 Mom was recruited with thousands of other women to work in the arms factory making bullets at first, graduating to making 500-pound bombs and finally on various aircraft that carried these bombs to be dropped over Germany. Everyone figured that if war ever broke out, it would be over and done within a few months and they would all go back to their families or find other jobs. Everything seemed to be normal for now, her father was even praising the likes of the Italian dictator Benito Mussolini or 'El Duce' as her father loudly and fondly called him. Mussolini's photo was proudly hanging throughout the farmhouse. He would often say that the world needed more men like El Duce, and he would sort things out if Hitler couldn't.

If he only knew Mom was now working for the other side.

As things have a way of happening, war started to escalate, and Mom went along to her new job working in a weapons factory. She was quickly put on the assembly line that made bomber and Spitfire aircraft and became one of the first of many women known as the famous 'Rosie the Riveters' doing their bit for the war effort. Her job was inserting red hot rivets into various parts of the aircraft she was working on and blasting them into position with her trusty pop-rivet gun fondly called 'Big Boy,' for reasons only known to her. She dyed her naturally blond hair to become overnight a flaming redhead. All her gal pals immediately nicknamed her 'Little Red' or just 'Red' after the fiery hot rivets she handled all the time. Mom was proudly featured in a short film and several newspapers about the patriotic women of America who, although were not able to use a real gun, had no problem with handling a 'pop-rivet' gun instead.

Eventually, a horrified Grandpa Enrico did find out that one of his daughters was working for the Allies and against his beloved Mussolini. 'Traditore!' (traitor) he shouted. He shortly passed away in 1943 age 68. Not so much from grief or anger but probably from too much moonshine liquor he haphazardly concocted from a still under the house.

Then one day Mom caught the eye of a Hollywood talent scout who was searching through the various war plants around the country for some ladies who looked like Hollywood stars and who wanted to make a fast buck. He spotted Mom and immediately thought her sultry looks were a dead ringer for the actress Bebe Daniels. However, Mom knew her talents lay not on a casting couch but in other areas. She wasn't the least bit interested in being a poor man's look-alike; she had her own ideas on entertaining the troops. When night-time came Mom and her gal pals would do their bit for the war effort but in their own special way.

When the quitting time siren went off it was time for the women to down their tools and clock off from the factory floor. Most went home but not Mom. She and some of her pals would high tail it out the door faster than anyone could clock off and quickly changed from plain old, drab 'Rosie's' into a glamorous USO (United Service Organisation) hostesses. Here, in a large hall coffee and refreshments were served. There was music and hostesses like Mom to keep the service personnel company. She was, by now, well and truly known as 'Little Red' the red-hot spitfire...a name she soon adopted. After all, if the boys couldn't have the real thing, I'm sure they didn't mind a red headed bombshell like Mom entertaining them.

Little Red was now becoming the most popular 'hostess with the mostess' serving coffee and donuts at the USO Canteen. They all enjoyed singing and dancing to the sounds of swing time such as Glen Miller, the boogie woogie music of the Andrew Sisters and other swing time tunes.

Now I'm not saying Mom had loose morals because she wasn't that kind of gal. She did find out early in life that she had a very healthy outlook on sex and to her it wasn't a dirty word. To her way of thinking if men could get away with having sex all the time then why not the women. It was just a fact of life and everyone did it, in her view.

For her it was a time to have some fun and be liberated. She would often smile to herself and think if they could only see her now back on the farm. Her father would have probably dropped dead from a stroke and her mother would have gone straight into a convent perpetually on her knees praying. No wonder she told me years later, when I was older, when the boys in the navy were due to be shipped out for action, that the 'action' they got (a cheeky wink) from her, always left the boys with a smile on their faces as she waved them goodbye from the docks. I suppose she too had her needs and desires like the armed forces did. After all there was a war going on and she figured she was doing her bit for the war effort. Later, she would nostalgically say that the war years were the happiest days of her life and volunteering in the USO was the best "job" she ever held down.

It was now early 1945 and everyone could see that the war would not last for ever and things were slowly winding down at the aircraft factory. Mom realized she would soon need a new job when eventually everybody like herself was finally laid off. She quickly found employment working in the 'Nu Laid' egg factory where she toiled non-stop, 10 hours a day, doing what was then called, 'kindling eggs.' The job was only deemed fit or suitable for women to do as their hands and fingers were considered more nimble and agile than those of a man. The job required each woman to hold two eggs per hand and twirl them or 'kindle' them around a very bright light bulb. They had to inspect the four eggs for any imperfections or defects that might be inside. The eggs that passed the light bulb test were then put on a conveyor belt and sent down to the packers and placed into the same type of cartons we know today. Speed and agility were essential in getting and maintaining a day's wage.

Some days were good and paid well but most of the time Mom was slowly falling behind the other women on the factory floor and she knew it. Her boss kept complaining and constantly harassing her by yelling in his thick Bronx accent,

"Yo Red! Ya not meeten ya target sweedhart, ya gotta pull ya finga out of ya fanny and woik harda and fasta! Ya droppin' too many god-damn eggs and ya slowen everybody down. Pick up your pace sweetcakes, make up the numbas or get you and ya keester (American slang for bum or ass) the hell out-a-here, ya capsiche!" (Italian slang for capisci meaning understand?).

Mom knew she was slowing down and seemed to be getting clumsier as she frantically worked faster with her egg kindling.

She dropped far more eggs than her manager ever knew about but never-the-less, she had to keep going on but knew what was happening to her hands and fingers and why they weren't doing what they were supposed to do. She had the early stages of Rheumatoid Arthritis in her fingers and hands. Mom knew her days were numbered if the manager ever discovered her problem. So, Mom had to come up with a plan fast that would hide her dropped eggs that were regularly accumulating around her feet and find a way of getting rid of the slippery evidence.

She figured, no evidence no crime.

One day as Mom was unpacking some groceries that were covered in wax paper when she had a 'light bulb moment'. Before they had plastic wrap, everyone used wax paper to keep things fresh. Why not get enough wax paper together and line my handbag with it? Then if she cracked, broke or dropped any eggs, she would simply scoop them up quickly and drop them in to her wax lined handbag. No fuss no muss and no one was ever the wiser from then on.

Her days and nights were now spent bent over her tiny light bulb, working what overtime she could get, kindling her eggs and sending them down the always hungry conveyor belt. She was able to maintain her quota, thanks to her wax lined handbag and consistently met any targets set by management. Mom did this job for another five years secretly hiding her dropped eggs and slipping them into her ever larger handbags.

Her boss never did find out what was going on.

Finally, the day came when all the women were replaced by mechanization, right down to that damn tiny light bulb. Mom's final shift at the plant came and as she clocked off for the last time kindling her eggs in 1955. However, mom wasn't quite finished with the egg business yet. She decided to steal a half dozen eggs and proceeded to slip them into her ever ready waxed lined handbag. Mom figured she may as well get something out of this place after all the years of hard work, little pay and listening to her boss drone on about her working so slow. Suddenly, mom spotted her boss's car, and in another light bulb moment, she waltzed up to his car and in an act of anarchy, cracked the entire half dozen eggs into his gas tank, shells and all.

Game set match to Little Red.

Mom's next job was sorting soft drink bottles into crates so they could be washed and reused. The job entailed lifting 20-pound crates (approx. 9 kilograms) filled with 24 bottles and sorting them into their correctly named crates. The heavy crates were mixed with Coke, Pepsi, Canada Dry and various other soft drink bottles. After they were sorted into their prospective named soft drink crates, they were then re-lifted onto a giant conveyor belt where they, like her eggs, went down to be washed and sorted. Like her last job, it was deemed that females were better at sorting than men, as speed was again the overriding factor in sorting the different bottles. The more bottles you sorted the more pay you received.

I think Mom's going to need a bigger handbag.

Chapter 3

BONES

After a never-ending string of lovers throughout the war years, Mom was beginning to worry that she would never find the true love and happiness that so many of her gal pals had found. These friends had a husband at the front or were seeing someone who was left behind. Her friends who had boyfriends or husbands who were overseas wrote copious amounts of love letters to them. Some had lovers that were so old and long in the tooth it didn't matter. Their motto was if you snagged a man and he's got a pulse then "Beggars couldn't be choosers, or you'll end up being a loser." The thought of ever finding a husband or someone to love seemed now as far away as the war was long. Mom had nothing to fall back on but the USO, and the USO days would soon become a faded memory. Further, she was aware her biological clock was ticking as the years rolled on.

Everywhere Mom looked she saw women wheeling around prams with babies or with children in tow. Mom had no letters, no babies and no romance on any horizon. Just work. All that seemed available to her were married men on leave, the dregs of men left behind or the men who would come into the night clubs she frequented looking for a good time with 'Little Red.' She was now approaching the age of twenty-seven and felt her youth and good looks along with the possibility of meeting Mr. Right and having a baby were slipping away. An unmarried woman closing fast on thirty was considered either a spinster or someone left on the shelf. The dreaded Spinster Shelf was fast approaching, and it meant only one thing for Mom and that it was a real possibility she just might end up perched high on it.

Then one fateful day one of her pals suggested Mom write to this guy who was still stationed somewhere called Attu, a lonely Aleutian Island of Alaska. Her friend said he was stationed with her husband, was single and in need of a friendly letter from any single woman that was alive and kicking. Mom was certainly alive and kicking so she jumped at the chance to write to this dashing man stationed out where the polar bears roamed. Mom was just the gal to comfort a lonely G.I out in God knows where on that tiny island called Attu, Alaska.

They wrote to one another and at first it was a casual exchange of cordiality but soon progressed to hot and steamy love letters that must have sent the Army Censor Board into salacious over-drive. Back during the war years, all letters either to or from the troops were routinely opened, read or always heavily censored by the Army Board of Censors. God forbid any secret war information about one's sex life should ever get into the hands of the Japanese or Germans. Mom often said the back-room censor boys had to get their jollies somehow by reading those steamy love letters from those sex-starved boyfriends stuck overseas, not to mention the replies from the sex-mad girlfriends left behind. By the time Mom finally got any letters from her 'new' boyfriend the actual letters looked more like the rats had eaten it away with just a few words here and there that one had to patch together to make a sentence or to make any sense from it. Usually you made do with a word here and there and made the rest up the way you wanted your letter to read or hoped it would have been before the Censor Board got a hold of it and chopped it all to pieces. Letters to my future Dad ended up the same way.

At long last, the war was slowly winding down there was some hope from Mom for them to finally get married. It was a dream come true for Mom but unknown to her at the time this 'lonely' G.I had been married a couple of times before. He was either still married or in the process of getting a divorce and had a string of love letters from other women to attest that he wasn't such a lonely GI marooned out in the Aleutians Islands after all. Apparently, it had escaped his attention to tell her these small details. However, my mother had more important things to worry about than these mere trivialities she didn't want to know about. She wanted to marry this guy who by now was taking up all her free time and money. She genuinely had fallen in love with him and she felt he had given her the same thing back. After the war ended Mom was front and centre waiting for him on the docks.

As they set up house, the days, weeks and months dragged on and on with still no hint of a trip to the altar. By now Mom was panicking that she would never get married to the one man she truly thought she loved or to have that much longed for baby. That dreaded shelf was still staring at her right in the face. Finally, in late 1946 Mom's dream of finally getting hitched came true. She married the man of her dreams and her first real love, my future father, 'Bones' in Reno Nevada.

Whether she had a shotgun in hand is debatable to this day.

After a very short time of wedded bliss it slowly began to dawn on her that she had married a 'no good stinking louse' and should never have gotten mixed up with him in the first place. He would be less of a father and even worse as a husband. "Desperation and panic make for bad judgement calls," she would later say. Her fantasy of wedded bliss and having a husband had well and truly evaporated.

My Dad had been married twice before and since Mom would now be number three, she thought, at first, she would certainly be his last. Not realising of course that he would have a string of long-lasting love affairs and be married at least two or three more times after her. 1950 was fast approaching but still she clung onto the hope of saving her marriage and of having that longed-for baby. But things were grim on both these fronts. Having an absent husband and now into her early thirties didn't improve her chances to successfully get pregnant. If you were in your thirties and still with no children, then you were most likely never going to have any. In those days, for women hitting thirty, it was considered too late or dangerous to even think of having children. Then one day in early 1950 at thirty-two years of age it finally happened. Mom was at last pregnant with me and I was born in November 14, 1950. She had hoped this must surely be the cure for her worries and save their troubled marriage.

However, it was not meant to be.

When my father heard the 'happy' news from Mom he flew into a vicious rage and beat her so savagely she was put immediately into the hospital on life support. The reports from the police and the doctors stated she took several heavy punches and kicks to her breasts, face and stomach and by this time was so badly disfigured it was hard to tell she was once actually human much less a woman that was pregnant. The doctors whispered that she looked like a wet papier Mache doll that had been badly moulded into human form. There was talk by the doctors she would most likely die or at best lose the baby within the next forty-eight hours. It depended on her strength and determination to pull through. Mom had other ideas and astonished the doctors by making a full recovery and keeping her baby. Dad, of course, cried copious amounts of crocodile tears and begged her for forgiveness saying it would never ever happen again. She believed him and took him back.

As in most cases, the lies and abuse never stopped.

In the early 1950's if you had a family you had everything, and you truly thought you at long last had made it in life. The dutiful wife stayed at home, looked after her adoring husband and children and was never expected to go out to work or make a living as that was the role of the devoted husband. It was even found slightly odd and going against the natural order of things to see a married woman working, making her own money. Stranger still, was for a woman to have a career instead of the joys of a family life. The woman of this lucky man would be provided for as his wish was her only real purpose in life and his command was her happiness to fulfil his every desire. Or so she thought and hoped for. After all, wasn't this how it was always portrayed on this invention called television? You can bet your last dollar this was never the case in our household. Mom had long ago given up any fantasies of trying to emulate the happy families she saw every night on TV. There was no point in making her husband a hot meal when he never showed up. No point in wearing an apron in stilettos and making a cocktail for someone who didn't appreciate it when he came home too late. Dear ol' dad was far too busy seducing all the women he could get his grimy little hands on, married or single, it just didn't matter to him. They were free for the taking and for him it was a veritable smorgasbord of women just waiting. It was the hunt and the final capture that he liked best. In some ways it was a relief for Mom as she had given up trying to please him and besides it kept him busy and away from the both of us and free from the beatings she was still enduring from time to time.

For him the hunting was far more exciting than being married.

My father loved to splash the cash about with the ladies and showing them a good time. He was one of the original 'Good time Charlies' of the world. He likened himself to be a real 'ladies' man' and his goal was to make love to as many women as he wanted. From all accounts he was extremely good at 'strutting his stuff.' Money for his girlfriends was top priority and he seemed to have plenty on hand to throw about, but to find money to feed his wife and child was another matter. It was constantly in short supply. Mom realised she was totally dependent on this dead-beat husband as she had been with the other men in her life. She was forbidden by him to find a job and was not allowed to go out anywhere unless given permission by him to do so. She was like an indentured servant, bound to the house and to him. No different from the farm life she had run away from when just eighteen. Often, she would beg him for some money to at least feed me as it was never a problem for her to go without food.

At times she was forced to swallow her pride and reluctantly beg for money from her family or her friends but mostly for any leftover food they might have. Dad didn't seem to worry as he was only concerned about the next conquest that was always on the horizon for him. He just didn't have any shame. Mom use to say, "Your Dad couldn't keep his fly done up much less keep his pants on." Nothing would stand in his way when it came to women, not even the woman or baby he left behind who went hungry. The bills started mounting up and become overdue. Then the threatening and abusive phone calls would start late at night and continue into the early hours. Calls were not only from debt collectors but also from husbands who found out what Dad was doing with their wives and they knew where he lived.

There were always angry people banging on the front door abusing Mom, looking for Dad, demanding money for an overdue account or to just punch his lights out. When the electricity and gas were finally was cut off, it was the final straw. Then to add insults to her injuries, the debt collectors came to the front door and proceeded to take away her own furniture. The furniture she originally bought and paid for was now being loaded onto a truck and carted away. Everything was eventually sold off to pay for the outstanding debts he had racked up in entertaining his girlfriends. I guess Mom soon realized it was the end of her fairy-tale story and it was time to wake up and smell the coffee. It was at long last, time for my father to face the music and his responsibilities, one way or the other. Mom was determined that he either mend his ways or he would pay for what he was doing to her.

That time came when Mom couldn't face the shame of her husband's behaviour. Enough was enough. One day she got a mysterious phone call from someone saying that Mom's good-for-nothing husband was spotted in the back seat of his car with another woman doing 'The nasty canasta' to the music of Doris Day warbling happily away on the car's radio. Mom slammed the phone down, grabbed a large meat cleaver from the kitchen drawer a heavy sledgehammer from the garage and an axe. She was going hunting and she knew exactly where to find her prey - her no good for nothing husband. Mom soon spotted dad's pride and joy, his 1952 Desoto car. She crept up behind the car like an animal stalking its prey to peek in the back window to see what was going on in the back seat of his now jumping car. As she got closer, she could hear the tell-tale moans and groans of two people in the grips of passion. Suddenly, up sprang a leg and then another one popped up with a pair of panties spinning around one ankle like a drum majorette twirling her baton on parade. All the time she kept in rhythm to the tunes of that damn Doris Day singing in the background. As Mom got closer to the car, she lifted her trusty and very heavy sledgehammer and let loose with a vengeance never seen in her before. At the top of her voice she let out a blood curdling and ear piercing screams any self-respecting psychopath would be proud to hear.

"You no-good two-timing son of a bitch!" she shrieked. "I'll fix your little red wagon once and for all!"

She opened the front door, snatched his keys away and promptly threw them into the river next to the car. Then without missing a beat and before they knew what the hell was about to hit them, Mom let out another deafening scream and promptly continued to smash the living daylights out of his prized car with her trusty sledgehammer. She proceeded to slam the heavy sledgehammer down onto the bonnet of the car whereby the weight of the hammer was now punching large but neat round holes through it. Next, she pulled out from her handbag her trusty axe which she used to hack into any metallic surfaces it encountered, namely the car doors. She then turned her attention to the steamed-up car windows and with great gusto smashed each one with the strength of a blacksmith on a mission from the almighty god Thor himself. Nothing outside or inside the car was spared as Mom swung her hammer and axe back and forth across his car. Then without missing a beat she swung open the badly hacked up front passenger's doors and started to chop the front seats up with her meat cleaver.

Mom was on roll and nothing was going to stop her reeking her revenge. The next thing she pulled out from her handbag of tricks was a large butcher's knife and began to stab all the tyres. Alfred Hitchcock himself would have been proud of her as she progressed from tyre to tyre turning them into shredded pieces of rubber, flattening them as flat as a proverbial pancake like some demented psycho loose baying for revenge. Mom kept merrily swinging, smashing, slashing and chopping away at the remaining surfaces with gay abandonment. Meanwhile the woman in the back seat was by now totally unhinged and shrieking in utter terror. After all, it's not every day your orgasm is so rudely interrupted by a crazy woman going nuts, and who by the looks of it is hell bent on committing mayhem or murder with a large meat cleaver in one hand and a sledgehammer in the other. Each time Dad's girlfriend would attempt an escape from the back seat, Mom would run around to her shrieking like a screaming banshee to warn this poor unfortunate woman of her impending fate after she finished with Dad's car. This only served to send dad's girlfriend completely hysterical.

By now Mom was finding her rhythm, beating the living daylights out of what was left of dear old dads now battered up car. Maybe she thought it was better than doing it to her husband since he loved that car more than he did his wife and child. The last thing Mom, dad and the neighbours saw was this poor demented woman crawling out of one of the shattered windows, running shrieking down the dirt track with her hands in the air and not a stitch of clothing on but her panties that were still twisted and firmly tangled around that one ankle. She apparently was never seen again. Now Mom set her sights on my dad who for once was lost for words and was cowering in the back seat like a small boy. He must have wondered what the hell had gotten into this once meek but now crazed woman he had married. I suppose he thought that she had lost her mind. She raced over to the back of the car where my dad was by now sitting bolt upright and for once paying her the necessary attention she commanded. She then proceeded to smash through the one remaining window still intact. The car, by now, looked like something out of a gangster movie that had just been machined gunned by the police. There was not a surface left on the car that was not dented, smashed or with some sort of hole in it. She leaned through the freshly smashed window and with her meat cleaver in one hand and the butcher's knife in the other, breathlessly said to my father "Now pack your bags and take your bony ass with them!"

From then on, his family and friends teased him by calling him by his new nickname, 'Bones.'

As she turned to walk away, she noticed something she had inadvertently missed in her earlier rampage. She walked back to the car, opened the front door and with a final "Shut the fuck up, Doris!" triumphantly swung her heavy hammer one more time straight into the dashboard radio, silencing Doris Day's warbling hits of the day once and for all. There now was nothing left that once remotely resembled his beloved Desoto car. We never saw or heard from him again. Mom finally found the courage, that had gone missing during those years of abuse, to, at long last, stand up for herself.

For now, there was nothing left to do but file for divorce and start over again. She would soon need all that courage, if she was going to survive.

After my mother divorced my dad, Bones, in 1953 she replaced her loneliness by numerous men who were always introduced to me as 'uncle.' They would come traipsing through our lives, but somehow, they would never stay longer than a month or two at best. I guess in hindsight a woman with a kid is just too much baggage for any man to take on. The upside of having so many 'uncles' for me was always getting presents, pieces of clothing, toys, shoes or some socks. The gifts were probably given from feeling guilty I suspect. I didn't mind as I liked the presents each new uncle would give me. Instead of receiving money from my uncles, Mom would ask for food or for them to buy something for the 'kid.' I chose to believe that hunger can make you do strange things in order to survive.

Mom also enjoyed the gifts from her boyfriends. Later in life she explained that she never accepted money from them as she considered this to be cheap.

The uncles would always leave her and once again, she would sink back into her despair at being left abandoned. She felt Mr. Right was never going to come along. When her Mr. Right finally came along and married her, she could not have been more wrong.

CHAPTER 4

THE BRIDES OF CHRIST

Early 1954

Before the monster came, Mom and I were once happy.

I am almost four years old and my day with Mom would always start like any other day in our house. We were living in what was then called 'The Housing Project Homes' and they were strictly for poor or low-income people. Usually single, divorced or abandoned women on welfare with children could benefit from this type of subsidised housing. My mother and I qualified in every way. Mom would get up every morning at 4 o'clock as she had been doing for years way before I came into this world. She would get me ready for our next-door neighbour Bobbie, who would come in to babysit me until Mom arrived home from work at the 'NuLaid Egg Plant' at 5pm.

Mom could not afford any real heating in our house so to remedy this she would often use her matches to light the gas oven stove in the kitchen to warm us up as we prepared for our day. I would patiently watch Mom striking several of her matches, anxiously waiting for the familiar 'pop' sound when the gas was finally ignited, bringing the oven suddenly to life. When it reached a certain temperature, she would turn the heat off, open the oven door and the heat would warm the house and everything would be nice and cosy.

After my morning bath, I would happily stand in front of the opened oven door as the warmth caressed my body while she gently dried me with a towel. When the warm air enveloped my small body, it was as if I was in a warm and comforting embrace. As the heat was warming both our bodies it gave off an aroma that was intoxicating to me and would always remind me of my mother's love. It was a blend of her strong unfiltered Camel cigarettes which she always had in her mouth and her trademark strong 'cowboy' coffee that was always brewing on the stove nearby. This heady aroma offered me a sense of comfort and a strong feeling of protection.

Back then we didn't have a care in the world. Life was good for the both of us.

However, on this morning, something was not quite right with Mom. I noticed she was not her usual calm and happy self but seemed distracted and slightly agitated by something. She was smoking incessantly and fidgeting with my clothes as well as hers. She was clearly nervous about something. Whatever it was, I would soon find out the reason.

As she checked herself repeatedly in the mirror, she casually stated "This is going to be a very special day for 'us' honey, your too big for a babysitter and would be going to a big boys' school now". I didn't understand what a school was as I was only four years old, so this was a complete mystery to me. Mom would only tell me to be patient and to wait and see. She would only say that it was going to be a big day for me with lots of other children being there with even bigger surprises. I had to look my best and I noticed Mom was also wearing her best clothes. She was wearing the suit that she wore at her wedding.

Mom asked me to "Please, please be on your best behaviour honey and to do everything the nuns tell you to do."

That's the first time I had ever heard that strange word.

"Nuns, what are nun's Mommy?" "Who are they?" "How long do I have to stay there?" "Will I still be able to play Cowboys and Indians there?"

"Never mind," she told me, "You'll find out soon enough."

Somehow, I took little comfort in her response to my questions.

We were about to be acquainted with one of the strictest and strangest Catholic Nursery Homes for children of poor, lower class families and single mothers. Unknown to the both of us, and to any other parent for that matter, this was without a doubt the last place any parent should have put their child.

The nuns who ran this institution were called 'The Convent of the Immaculata.' Outwardly they looked the part of what they were supposed to do, that is, taking care of vulnerable young children. However, they were not only grossly unfit to run a nursery school but were ill equipped and totally unqualified to care for small children between the age of four and five years. Today I would have no hesitation in calling it a sect had it not been for the fact is was in the guise of a Catholic institution.

Mom was given strict instructions over the phone by a very haughty sounding Mother Superior to be at the school gates for enrolment promptly at 6 am. It was made very clear that if we were late, I would not be allowed to be enrolled and would not be eligible for any enrolments later in the year. If I was to be accepted into their school, then Mom was never, ever to be late when I was dropped off at the front gates or when being picked up.

Mother Superior then finished in a menacing tone, "Tardiness," she droned on, "Will not be an acceptable excuse and if you are late for admission your child will not be let into the yard. Do I make myself clear? Once the iron gates are closed, they will not be opened again. If you are ever late for morning roll call, your child will be barred from entry and sent home. Do I make myself understood, Madame?"

"Yes, Mother Superior, I do." Mom then bent down and kissed Mother Superior's large ruby ring on her right hand and left.

God forbid if that should ever happen as we would have to go back home, forcing Mom to take a day off work which she could ill afford being the sole bread winner. Mom would often say to me that poverty was a great equalizer and to never be ashamed of it. I didn't understand what poverty was then but in hindsight I never ever thought we were poor or needy. Mom meekly agreed and soon we were hurrying along the still dark streets on an unseasonably cold September morning. I found it difficult keeping up with Mom in her haste to meet the nun's deadline for enrolment.

I was four years old and we were running late.

We finally arrived breathless at the school to find ourselves rushing up a long dark, winding, gravel pathway that led up to a large multi storied unlit grey building surrounded by a massive brick wall. Years later it reminded me of something out of a Charles Dickens novel I once read. As we breathlessly walked up to the imposing wall, we were confronted by two enormous iron gates with two strange and frightening looking creatures perched on either side. Mom said they were 'gargoyles' and were used to protect people from evil. As we came to a stop, I could hear Mom trying to catch her breath, gasping, "God I hope we're on time, and while you're at it help me give up smoking too.".

Unfortunately, we were on time.

As she took her hands out of her pocket, I noticed Mom was shaking un-controllably. She took one last drag from her cigarette whilst reaching for the large bell to ring for someone to let us into this dark, secluded and imposing building.

"Where are we Mommy?" I whispered. I felt an odd chill run through me as it carried my breath away. "Please can we go home now Mommy?" Mom was still breathlessly saying to this god, "I hope we are not late." We would soon find out.

Just then I heard coming from the school a very loud bang. It was like a door being caught by the wind and suddenly slamming shut. As I was looking through the gate, I noticed a very odd sight. Coming toward us was a strange person oddly dressed from head to toe in black and white, running frantically toward the gates as if they were being chased by the devil himself. As this creature got closer, it suddenly appeared to slow down, their black and white costume was gently billowing in the wind. It now seemed as though they were floating down the path in slow motion. Oh, how wonderful it all looked and seemed so beautiful and serene.

In the early morning light, she seemed almost angelic in nature as she moved gracefully up to the front gates. However, as she came closer into view, I was horrified at what was about to greet us. There standing before us was not a beautiful angelic like creature but something that had morphed into the shape of an old and haggard woman - a woman that was completely covered up from head to toe in black and white with only her withered and deeply lined face showing. And she had whiskers!

So, this is what a nun looks like I thought.

When she finally reached the gates, I noticed she clutched a cane in one hand. She seemed to prop or steady herself with the cane whilst digging deep into her costume with the other hand to pull out an enormous metal key. She, at once, shot us a condescending look as her eyes darted back and forth. We felt there were other eyes watching her to make sure she did everything correctly. I could see her piercing eyes inspecting us, especially me, as she looked us both up and down and with a sneer of utter contempt as she laid her cane down against a nearby tree. Suddenly, she outstretched both her pale and bony hands that seemed to magically materialize from underneath the black drapery that covered her.

She grabbed the gate with both her hands and slowly inserted her key into the iron lock. With some difficulty she at last managed to turn the key to unlock the massive gates. As she was trying to do this, I couldn't help but notice that her hands were unusually translucent, with bulging veins criss-crossing them. With a loud clank the gates crept apart as the nun struggled with their weight. Once opened, we hesitantly stepped inside. As we made our way through the entrance the gates started to pick up speed to close as if by magic. Mom, in a vain attempt to help close the gates, was met by the harsh voice of the nun,

"Stop!" she hissed through her yellow stained teeth, "I need no help from the likes of you."

It suddenly slammed shut behind us with an almighty crash.

Once closed I could see that all views of the outside world were now well and truly blocked. This was a private and secret world. That's how they like it.

I quickly glanced back to see the staring gargoyles still sitting on their perches as if waiting for their next victims or meal to arrive. Up the gravel pathway we went and as I got closer, I could see more of these strange people in black and white robes nervously waiting for us. Some were in the playground watching us as they paced back and forth, others stared ominously down at us from the many windows of the school. Some were pointing at us as we all gathered in the school courtyard.

I instantly had a familiar chill come over me. At the same time, I unconsciously started to pull Mom backwards in a futile attempt to leave this frightening place.

"Mommy, I want to go home. I don't like it here. I'm scared."

Nervously Mom said, "Don't be silly honey, everything's going to be okay. You'll see."

I was not convinced as she dragged me closer to the nuns. They were by now gathering in ever increasing numbers to meet the newcomers and their parents. I could see that all these strange creatures were standing at rigid attention as if on guard duty. They appeared to be impatiently looking and nervously waiting for something to happen. But what, I thought?

They weren't the only ones nervous that day.

Back in the 1950's, if you were a Catholic parent, it was your implied sacred duty to obediently hand over your children to these awaiting nuns without hesitation.

More and more nuns were now coming into view and could be seen in their immaculately starched uniforms with a smug imperious look etched onto their withered old faces. Others suddenly appeared from nowhere as if by magic looking nervous and seemingly not knowing what to do with themselves at the sight of so many children. I could see the nuns were clutching and clicking noisily with some strange wooden beads that were attached to their waists and hanging down their sides, silently mouthing words. Some paced back and forth whispering to one another covering their mouths so as not be heard as they nervously glanced at us.

I later found out these beads they wore were reverently referred to as Rosary Beads that hung around their waists with a very large wooden crucifix attached to the end of them. Apparently the more important you were, entitled you to a larger and more ornate crucifix. Others kept their hands and arms secreted inside their voluminous black long-sleeved robes, making them more frightening as they appeared to have no hands or arms when they floated by muttering to one another in a strange language only they understood.

As we were being led up the rest of the path the nun who was ushering us into the compound suddenly stopped in her tracks, turned around, and with her gnarled bent index finger held it up to her mouth and hissed through her crooked yellow stained teeth, "Talking is no longer permitted from this point onwards."

"Children will speak only when spoken to!"

She stated in a no-nonsense manner, that all things must go through the Mother Superior. Apparently, this person appeared to know all and see all in her domain - (whatever and whoever a Mother Superior was). As I cautiously searched their faces gazing down at us through the many windows and doorways, I could see from where I was standing that they didn't look very happy. Unbeknown to us, we had penetrated their mysterious domain. It certainly appeared they didn't like our intrusion. That cold chill came over me again with an uncomfortable sensation that we were not at all wanted or welcomed here.

Everything was not what it appeared to be.

Mom and I did our best to blend in with the other mothers and children nervously waiting nearby. I couldn't help but wonder which one was the Mother Superior that Mom had been talking about or to find out what a Mother Superior was in the first place. As I timidly looked about, I noticed the years had not been kind to any of the nuns. They seemed old, skinny and quite frail looking. The nuns seemed polite to the faces of each parent whom they had to meet and greet, especially to the paying ones as they were deemed more valuable to their needs. They were given coffee and cake and their children received a cookie. For the children of the parents who couldn't afford to pay, their children received nothing on admission day, but a certain type of 'special' treatment was awaiting them.

There would be no coffee or cake for us on that day.

To say the nuns were the masters of deception would be an understatement. They knew how to put on a good show for the parents to make them feel that each child was special, and their welfare was important to them. Did the parents not realize or appreciate that their child would now be cared for and be in the best of god's hands? After all, was it not the calling for each nun to do the Lord's work and care for these children of fallen, single or divorced women? In their twisted minds, looking after a divorced woman's child was bad enough but for the mothers who had their child out of wed lock was something the nuns could not tolerate.

Unwed mothers had committed the ultimate sin against the Church in the eyes of the nuns. Divorce, similarly, was unacceptable in their beliefs and was considered a stain against the sacred bonds of matrimony. Being a divorced Catholic woman, like my mother, was considered a gross offence against the Catholic Church.

It was as if Mom had slapped the Mother Superior herself.

The child of such 'crimes' against God and the nuns would indeed warrant their special attention. Soon the nuns would decide which children needed this 'special' treatment.

It would appear my redemption was at hand.

As each parent kissed, hugged and bade their sobbing child goodbye, the parents would be hurriedly ushered out through the reopened iron gates. I doubt any of them suspected what would soon be happening to their child. The parents blindly trusted and naively believed in the spiritual side of the Catholic Church's indoctrination. None of the parents had the slightest worry about leaving their child in the care of such a holy institution. After all it was run and operated by women who professed to be 'The Brides of Christ.'

The gates once again slammed shut with a deafening crash, cutting everyone off from the outside world. As soon as this was done the same nun who let us in now locked the gates with her trusty key. Now as if on an invisible and unspoken cue, all the nuns immediately swung into action. Each nun would instinctively know that the coast was now clear, and all bets were off.

No one saw in, no one saw out. We were now alone.

"Welcome to the Convent of the Immaculata" thundered across the loudspeaker. "Sisters, into your positions at once!"

The game was over, and it was show time.

As the nuns oversaw their domain again, they all turned towards us, the smiles that were put on for the parent's benefit had now been ominously wiped off their ugly faces and replaced with a look of self-righteous indignation. They now descended on us like a pack of hungry wolves, scrutinising each one of us with a look of abject contempt and disdain.

Did I just hear a nun say, "Oh, that one's mine?"

As children, we instinctively held each other's hands and closed ranks in the mistaken belief we were forming a protective barrier against what was now swiftly coming towards us. Terror quickly overcame each one of us as we saw different things etched into the nuns faces as they came closer to us to claim their 'prizes.' Some would come up to us and for no apparent reason, flick our ear lobes with their fingers and make condescending remarks to us as they walked by surveying their new "play-things."

They would grab hold of our faces, yank and squeeze them into some hideous deformity, turning our faces from side to side and inspecting us as if we were a kind of trophy they had just won. Others tugged and poked at our clothes to gauge the level of our personal hygiene. It seemed as though the nuns were deciding 'Which one do we get to play with and torment the most? Which one can we torture the most into submission, and which one would cause us the least or most trouble?' Some nuns could be seen smirking and giggling at us like little schoolgirls do when seeing a boy pass by for the first time.

They were in complete control now. These creatures, that called themselves nuns, felt they had the power to control and do whatever they wanted to do with these tiny dirty urchins who were intruding on their precious time. We were only four and five years of age and we presented as shabbily dressed, un-washed and generally looking like most children do who come from a poor background. I was only four at the time but knew I had holes in my shoes that I tried desperately to hide. My pants were worn away so you could see my knees, and like most poor kids, we probably smelt, confirming our poverty. However bad things might have looked, we were all happy little children and knew nothing about being poor. That was our lot in life and knew no different.

Today, our first day, our lives descended into a hell that no child was prepared for and from which there was no escape.

Each nun had the ability to target and single out the weak children from the pack. They managed to exploit any misdemeanour that might occur and to use any means of discipline they saw fit with the utmost severity. I found out later why there were no other children older than five years of age in this institution. Apparently, they took only the young ones as it was easier and safer to control them and their behaviour. Any child older than five years was thought by them to be too dangerous, to manage and control.

Control for the nuns was paramount for their own survival.

And children do talk.

The last thing the nuns wanted or needed was for a young child to do just that, talk, and worse, to be heard and believed by any adult. For the nuns to be questioned by anyone other than her fellow nun or having to explain their actions would be beneath their dignity and an insult to their station in life.

And that would never do.

Our first command was that all talking would now cease and hence-forth not tolerated under any circumstances. Silence and secrecy were their code, and no one was going to change any of that.

Noncompliance was at your peril.

Next we were forcefully dragged away screaming in terror by our 'respected nuns' each had claimed their various 'prizes.' I was gripped with an overriding sense of panic, helplessness and entrapment. I suddenly understood there was no escape for any of us. Mom once told me that each nun was especially chosen by God as his personal 'Bride' and she was his wife on earth making her a "Bride of Christ" which made them extra special to look after children like me. At first this made me feel quite special. I had a new babysitter who was married to this man named God.

I once asked my Mom "What's a God Mommy? Is he going to be my new babysitter?"

At the time God, Jesus and the pantheon of saints was a complete mystery to me or to any of the young children with me that day.

We find ourselves in this institution run by elderly women, who for all intents and purposes were married only to this 'God.' They not only hid behind a veil but behind an impenetrable wall of secrecy. All the time they were believing themselves to be pious, chaste and upstanding women all chosen by 'him.' In fact, I doubt that any of the nuns who 'looked' after us had any training or qualifications in dealing with children or the care of them. They were nuns after all and believed they were doing God's good work. Since God was on their side, that's all that was needed.

The brutal fact of the matter was that they were perhaps the least qualified group of people to care for innocent children. They were brutal, sadistic and cruel and should never have been given the chance to care for any of us. We were subjected to their endless idiosyncratic whims, taunts and cruelties. Attending that school and being subjected to their 'care', we never saw any acts of kindness, a sincere smile or anything to indicate a caring environment. Although they did have an uncanny ability to make you feel grateful for any small Moment of happiness that might come your way. If it did come your way you soon learned to be grateful and humble that it came from them and only them. God forbid if you ever forgot to say, "Thank you Sister" or a quick whipping from their dreaded rosary beads would be coming your way.

They droned on and on that we should feel blessed and honoured that we were with them, after all, they were the anointed ones chosen by God to care for us.

They would chant in unison: "God has sent you to us so we can save your mortal and wicked souls. We are the only ones who can save your miserable and sinful souls from the fires of hell. In us and only through us you will find eternal salvation in our never-ending war against the dark angel, Lucifer."

At various times of the day they would order us to get on our knees and give thanks to god for our safe deliverance to the nuns who were ready to save our wretched souls from the devil and his fiery furnace of hell.

Lucifer, popes, dark angel, furnace of hell, souls, war and damnation?

And so, my Catholic indoctrination began.

CHAPTER 5

THE LUNATIC ASYLUM

7:00 am.-7:30 am.

From now on our days would be strictly regimented by the nuns. We were not considered children anymore, not even students, but 'charges,' although I'm sure they had other names they muttered under their breath to describe us. Everything that was inside those walls had to be run like a well-oiled machine. Timing was always the essence for them in everything they did. No child, no matter how young or old, would be allowed to interfere with or alter their unbending routine.

There was absolutely no talking, laughing, or playing once inside the building, and tardiness was dealt with by a swift hard slap over your ears or a quick and painful rap over the head with their ruler or walking cane. Silence for them meant order and order it would be from now on in our new existence. We had no choice in the matter, and we were too scared to complain.

We learned from day one that each step we took had to also match their step which was controlled by the constant rhythmic tapping tempo against their hands of their rulers or from the bamboo staffs they carried with them when they walked by. They spoke in measured tones and did everything as one unit. If we ever unconsciously did something against their routine, the nuns had one special way of dealing with anyone who stepped out of line or caused a disruption. They would grab us by their hands in a choke hold and literally throw us into the infamous 'cupboard.'

The cupboard was in another room far away from the other children and remote enough so your cries and screams could not be heard by anyone. It was a dark cupboard-like closet without any windows, about the size of an average broom closet but big enough for a small child to squeeze into. A nun would drag you by the arm, kicking and screaming, open the doors and you would be shoved in head-first. Once inside the door would be securely bolted closed. As the closet was small and cramped you had to sit cross-legged or in a hunched position with your knees up by your chin. You could yell, scream and bang on the back of the door into the pitch black all you wanted but no one ever heard due to its remote location. When the time came you were grudgingly released by some sombre looking nun who thought you had reached a certain level of contrition.

From their point of view, it was a place to contemplate the error of your ways until you had served your penance.

"Have you asked God's grace for his forgiveness?"

"Yes sister," I would always say through gritted teeth.

Chalk up another lie and another sin. I'm on the road to hell.

Some days I would be dragged kicking and screaming to this dark closet and made to stay there for hours for something I had done or from some sin only known to by this nun. I would be given no food, water or the use of a toilet. However, once inside the darkened cupboard, I oddly felt safe and secure being away from everyone. This gave me an opportunity to figure out ways to survive this hell and avoid the nuns at the same time.

It was common knowledge that independence would not be tolerated and that beatings would be mandatory for any transgressions. Each new day our unsuspecting and blissfully unaware Moms would dutifully drop us off to the eager and smiling nuns waiting to see us again. Once the mothers were out of sight, all the fake niceties were no longer required. At 7 am. one hundred and fifty children were herded in strict formation into a very large auditorium, like cattle to the slaughter, to be served a small bottle of cold milk.

The auditorium itself was always kept brutally cold and airless with multiple lots of burning candles everywhere in the room. The smell and smoke they emitted was suffocating and truly nauseating. To this day I hate scented candles, soaps or incense of any kind. Inside, I noticed there were fifteen long, weathered wooden tables and Kenches with each table sitting exactly ten children with a nun sitting at the head. For the nuns, everything had to run like clockwork with no deviations or delays in the process of finding where we were supposed to sit.

You never kept a nun waiting for anything.

Across the room you could hear some of the nuns screaming out their orders "Hurry up there! Be quick about it! No talking!" "You're a stupid boy? Be quick now, I told you before, no talking!" On and on it went throughout the morning until we finally found the seats, we were supposed to occupy.

Once we finally had found our seats, one of the nuns stood before us on a podium and thundered that from now on we will remember our seat number. How we were supposed to do this when none of us could even count much less read would be anyone's guess. Whilst sitting we were told under no circumstances never to get off our seats or fidget. Talking was now forbidden and all our eyes must now be face forward and look at a blackened wall.

With all these new rules, it seemed to border on mass confusion for all the children as the nuns constantly screamed their orders. One minute we would blindly rush and go one way only to be screamed at to go the other way.

Our descent into bedlam quickened and was now on a grand scale.

At first, due to the dim lighting, we hadn't noticed anything unusual. However, as our eyes slowly became adjusted to the lighting, we all at once noticed a huge wooden cross hanging on the wall directly over the nun with a partially naked man stuck to it. I didn't realise who or what was happening to him. But to our horror it became evident this man was nailed to this cross and that his face and body were drenched in copious amounts of blood. A collective gasp could be heard across the room at seeing this grotesque spectacle and some of the children cried witnessing such a horrific sight.

Later in life I realized and believed it to have been a well-choreographed event to maximize the effect in shocking us into submission. It certainly worked. Back then I didn't understand why this was happening to this man. What did he do to deserve this I wondered? Was he a bad man and does this happen to everyone who is bad here? The nuns scrutinised our reactions as they strutted up and down the aisles with great determination etched on their lined faces. All that was left for them was the constant reminder and resentment of having to look after these young and innocent 'things' they called charges that they really didn't want to care for in the first place.

It reminded me of a prisoner of war movie I once saw, except, in this scenario, the nuns were armed with rulers and sticks - not guns. However, at this stage, I wasn't altogether sure they didn't have them under all that black material anyway.

They did have something in their arsenal that was equally as painful. Around their thin, pinched waistline was wrapped a wide leather belt and on the end of this belt hung large beads with an equally large wooden crucifix dangling at the end of it. Later, I was to realise these were the nuns' personal rosary beads. The leather belt was easily detachable and could be used at a Moment's notice to swing with great speed and strength for striking at the legs of some poor unsuspecting child. The beaded rosary belt with the cross was employed for maximum affect across any part of the body they saw fit to use it on.

The nuns, however, were extremely careful where they struck or hit any child as the last thing they wanted was to be questioned by a 'foolish' parent about any marks on their child's body. To be questioned by a parent was well beneath their dignity to answer, much less having to justify, and unthinkable for a parent to dare ask. The art of lying was not beneath them if they felt justified in doing so. After all who would believe a mere child over a nun's story about how he or she got the welts across their legs anyway? They would simply dismiss it by saying the child had a mishap in the playground. The nuns would sweetly tell the parents how children can be at play time. "Boys will be boys," they would say as they ominously stared in our direction.

There were never any questions. End of story.

Up and down they would strut, forever on the lookout for someone to make the slightest mistake or to step out of line. They had a look on their faces as if to say, "Go on, just try it once and see what happens to you." Like a cat playing with a mouse. On and on they went, watching and waiting for any infringement, large or small, of their rules. At times the nuns seemed almost eager for something to go amiss. Any mistake on our part would be enough of an excuse for them to come down on us like the pack of hungry animals. Back and forth they would go, pushing through groups of children, herding and flushing out the weaker ones. Randomly swinging their rosary beads as the screams would ring out across the large room as some poor, unsuspecting child was being lashed across the legs with something from their arsenal. Some of the children just held their ears to block out the now familiar screams.

Their eyes seemed to be everywhere, constantly darting about never missing an opportunity for any slip-up one of us might make. And slip-ups were often made. For example, if one of us were caught fidgeting or whispering. Such behaviour would incur a swift response by the nuns such as her leather strap being slammed down onto the desk barely missing the child's hand. If they couldn't find something, they would home in on the known weaker ones who were always an easy target. You could always hear some of the children whimpering or crying in the background or see them cowering in some far-off corner of the school. They were always the most vulnerable and the easiest of targets to work on. The nuns knew the weak ones were too afraid to complain and would always keep their mouths shut.

Besides, who's going to bother listening to dumb children anyway?

Control was now the name of the game and everything was in place for them to maximize it. Most of the time, we never knew what we were being punished for or when it was coming. Everything was always so unexpected many of us developed nervous twitches, wet our pants, developed a profound stutter or had learning difficulties later in life.

By the time I left at 5 years of age I had developed a crippling stutter when I entered a state-run school. This stutter set me back years until I was relentlessly coached by a sympathetic teacher who helped me finally overcome my affliction.

Some days all seemed quiet and going well with everyone minding their own business. Suddenly you would hear a blood-curdling scream from across the room and before you knew what was happening, you witnessed a child being wrenched out from their seat by their ear and out of class to be punished or made to stand up in front of class and be accused of doing something wrong. It never mattered to the nuns what you did or didn't do. Half the time we certainly didn't know ourselves. It soon became obvious it was pointless protesting one's innocence or begging the nuns for help because they were always right, and you were always wrong.

As each nun walked her beat, I started to notice some subtle differences. Each one had her own peculiar traits and idiosyncrasies. Some played nervously with their crucifixes; others would vigorously twirl theirs around like they were a band majorette twirling a baton. At times you could hear a kind of whirring noise as they spun their rosary beads through the air. I used to think they looked more like airplane propellers about to take off. Sometimes the nuns could be heard muttering strange words as they went about their daily duties. I used to think they were reciting some magical spell or incantation as they floated on by. Whenever the children caught them muttering such things to themselves and they saw us watching them, they would suddenly cease.

One thing they had in common, was that they carried a large wooden ruler they would constantly use to smack nervously against the inside of their palms. At times this ruler was a readymade weapon and was used to great effect on any unsuspecting child's backside or hand for a sin they allegedly committed. Others preferred their metre-long bamboo walking stick that was used with gusto on the backs of our legs and buttocks.

The nun who 'looked after me' was named Sister Enunciata. She preferred a leather strap she kept secreted in a pocket deep inside her robe. One minute your head would be down pretending to be in deep prayer and the next sound you would hear would be a loud crack coming down on your desk, just missing your hands.

"You, Boy! That was your first and last warning."

A warning for what? We were always asking ourselves what we had done wrong.

In the end, it was always easier to just say, "I'm sorry sister" or "Please forgive me sister I won't do it again." "Please don't hit me sister." "I'm sorry, I'm sorry."

We never knew why we were being punished and never knew when it was coming. Besides, we were too scared to ask. Anyone who did not reverently bow down low enough for them as they walked past would end up paying for it with an overzealous nun giving you a "thrashing of your life" with her trusty bamboo cane.

We were always looked down on by them as wicked and evil little things. In their sick and twisted minds, we had to be punished for all the sins we had committed, were committing now, and most assuredly will commit in the future. For show and to maximize the effect, punishment was by means of a beating with the crucifix, ruler or bamboo stick and in most cases in front of other children. After all, an audience was always used for maximum affect in controlling the masses.

Theatre was an important part of their control.

Apart from the nuns all looking the same there was another thing they had in common, they all walked in the same manner. They walked in strict military precision as if on parade, almost robotic in nature. You could hear someone in their group tapping out rhythmic cadences from their trusty bamboo rod either on their hands or hitting it onto the concrete floors. 'Tap, tap, tap', as they marched along the hallways. Left, right, left, right as they slowly glided by. Each nun had one overriding purpose in her life. This was to serve her husband, her god. One of my new friends whispered to me "Are we ever going to meet this man called God and who exactly is he anyway?"

If you were smart enough, you could pick up on the certain traits and peculiarities of each nun. You could use this talent to work the system to your advantage. I learned very quickly which ones to avoid at all costs. We were ordered to keep our heads bowed in reverence whenever a nun walked by, especially if it was Mother Superior. Not to do so meant a quick slap across your face or hard work scrubbing the floors, cleaning toilets, dusting or washing the many windows around the school and church. At times it seemed we spent more time working at our chores than sitting in a classroom learning about God, Jesus and all the saints.

Of the nuns at the school the worst one was the sadistic Mother Superior also known as Sister Bernadette. She had one shoe larger than the other and walked with a pronounced limp. She was feared by all, including the nuns I suspected, and was to be avoided at all costs.

I learned later she had a club foot and that she was born with this disability. The tell-tale sign she was approaching was the squeaking noise her metal shoe brace made; as she walked down the hallway along with her cane tapping on the floor. Her cane was always used to either steady herself or for beating some unsuspecting child she happened to come across. These sounds were an early warning of her approach; a signal for the rest of us to scatter and hide or if we couldn't get away fast enough, to fake being busy cleaning or reverently praying in some corner.

Sometimes she would come upon you so quickly you had just enough time to drop to your knees and pretend to be in deep spiritual prayer. It must have seemed rather odd to the other nuns to see all these children praying at the most peculiar times of day on bended knees facing blank walls, open doors or praying looking at a tree.

I'd pray to a mop and bucket if it got me out of a beating from her.

Sister Bernadette's face was now marked by years of blind obedience and servitude to God. If there was ever a hint of kindness or loving nature to her it had long since withered away. With her limp came a crooked back making her stoop over at an angle which must have made it even more painful for her constant kneeling, genuflecting and praying. One of her favourite punishments was to lock you away in the now infamous dark cupboard that I had already been acquainted with earlier. Another involved her making you hold heavy Bibles over your head in front of the class. If you dared drop any, as we invariably did due to the weight of them, she would slap you continuously with her hands across your ears causing a strange buzzing sound that stayed with you for the rest of the day.

All nuns bowed reverently to her as she walked by as if she was the holiest of icons. I still wonder if it was more in fear than respect that prompted such behaviour. I dare say the former would be closer to the truth.

She was a woman who ruled with an iron fist. A fist that was forever clutching her rosary beads.

CHAPTER 6

MY SALVATION BEGINS

7:30 am.- 8:30 am.

This was the time of day set aside by the nuns deemed the most important hour for the salvation of our wicked souls. We were constantly harangued all the waking hours of the day that we were going to hell for the sins we had committed. How a child that young could commit so many sins could only be known to the nuns and priests. The "fires of hell" are where we are all destined to go when we die.

Or so the nuns kept telling us and that's what the Bible kept telling them.

One day we were all herded into a classroom and made to sit upright and be perfectly still because a special guest priest had come all the way from Ireland to talk to us. His name was Father O'Brady. The nuns were in a flap as the overseas guest speaker was a big event. It was an honour for them that he should speak at their insignificant school. None of us had the slightest idea where or what Ireland was and cared little about it. The nuns were literally flying from room to room with flowers, papers and religious statues hurriedly placing them all over the rooms. They couldn't have done more if the Pope was coming.

After a while our room looked more like a funeral parlour than a classroom.

For us, it was more trepidation than excitement because we had no idea what a priest was. This was the first time we had heard that word. To me it meant another hour of tedious and boring lectures by someone on the virtues of the Catholic Church.

We were startled to see a man crash through the classroom doors, barely able to regain what dignity he had left, after he nearly fell face first onto the floor. So here we have our Irish priest all the way from Ireland who at first glance was clearly a burnt-out old man who showed little to no interest in the wellbeing of our souls much less in the teachings of the Catholic Church. When he began to speak, we immediately noticed a strong and overpowering smell that began to permeate our room. The combination of liquor, stale cigarettes and bad body odour fouled the unusually overheated and airless room around us as he dramatically emphasized every word with his orange and yellow stained fingers. The more he gesticulated and swayed with his arms and hands the more his fetid smell spread throughout the room.

Furthermore, his broad Irish accent along with his state of inebriation virtually made his speech incomprehensible to the class.

Today, he was going to talk about some family called Adam and Eve who apparently were the first people on this planet. They had two sons called Cain and Abel. All four of them lived happily ever after in a place called 'The Garden of Eden' until one-day God caught someone eating some fruit from a tree. By now, like most days, we all daydreamed of happier times and tended to zone out or stare straight into space. From what I picked out of the story so far seemed pleasant enough about a family living happily in a garden of some sort and I was lulled into a false sense of relaxation.

My first mistake of the day was to ask this priest what the fruit was.

"Was the fruit an apple, pear or an orange?" I asked?

"You're a stupid insolent boy aren't you because no one knows what type of fruit it was so don't ask me anymore asinine questions."

'Did he just say a swear word?' I thought to myself.

My second big mistake of the day, which wasn't going well in the first place, was to ask how Adam and Eve's two boys could make babies.

"How was that possible father?" "Can two boys have babies?" I asked.

Even at the age of four I was no dummy. I didn't know where or how you got babies but knew they couldn't come from two guys named Cain and Abel. Let's see father get out of this one. The priest spun around and locked a glare on me with a stunned look of horror at my daring to ask such an impertinent question. With the pent-up anger and frustration of years of not knowing the answer himself screamed out,

"Blasphemer! How dare you question me or the teachings of the holy Bible?"

He ran up to me, picked me up with both hands by my throat, and threw me onto the floor in front of the class. As I gasped for breath, I tried to pick myself up off the floor. He ran over to me and grabbed me again by the throat, lifting me high up into the air, dangling me about the classroom like a limp rag doll, while all the time screeching with rage that this is what he does to wicked little boys who will be destined for hell.

As he held me close to his bulging blood-shot eyes and screamed, all I could smell was his rank body odour and the stale cigarettes as I tried to catch my breath. As he swung me around the room, his spit hit my face as if it was coming from a viper itself. His face was crimson, with beads of sweat now pouring down his face and into his open mouth. By now many in the class were either screaming or crying in horror and disbelief. Some had wet themselves while others lost control of their bowels at seeing this spectacle unfold before their eyes.

Father O'Brady slammed me down onto the floor again and ordered me to hold both my hands out like Jesus did while he was being nailed to the cross. He then took a strap out of a desk and proceeded to beat me across the inside of each of my hands with five strokes. All the time he was bellowing and yelling for us to "Shut the hell up or the lot of you will get the same." He then raised me one last time very close to his sweaty face and whispered in a low and sinister voice,

"You little shit. In the future, you will be asking me for a quick and merciful punishment that would surely await you here or in hell."

After a few minutes of enduring this excruciating pain the bell mercifully began to ring just in time to save me for my next adventure into hell. He then threw me back onto the floor and Kent over me as I was sobbing and whispered into my ear,

"Boy, I'm not finished with you yet. I will happily await to see you again when you least expect me."

By now I was looked upon as a troublemaker by the nuns and therefore in need of extra attention. I may as well have had a target on me from then on. I was not only avoided by some of the children but for punishment was made to scrub clean all the school's toilets for a week - my 'penance.'

CHAPTER 7

BLUE BIRDS AND YELLOW FLOWERS

8 am.- 9 am.

This time of the day we were marched into the toilet area for instruction on how to use the toilet properly.

Mom had already trained me, so I knew how to use the toilet by myself. I knew what had to be done and where to do it but never-the-less the nuns were insistent on re-training us in the proper art of using a toilet. We were forced to go along with the younger or less experienced boys and girls to the toilet. The nuns would drag reluctant boys and girls by the arm to the toilet bowls or urinals whether you had to go or not. They barked

"Now go and hurry up, I haven't got all day with the likes of you filthy brats!"

If there was no evidence of you having gone to the toilet, the nuns simply whipped you with their Rosary beads on your bare backside for wasting their precious time.

I had never seen or been to a urinal before because I always used the toilet at home. This thing in front of me was completely foreign and left some of us slightly bewildered on how to use it properly. Do I sit in it or wash my hands with the water coming from it? I wondered. To top it off one of the nuns said someone would be coming in to show us the correct way on how little boys go to the toilet.

You can imagine our surprise when in marched this very old nun to demonstrate to the boys the correct procedure on how to use the urinal. The way she started to yank and pull up her voluminous habit to try and demonstrate to the boys the proper way of urinating into the urinal is something I will never forget. She started to show the boys the correct way to urinate in a flamboyant pantomime. She began by showing us how to unzip her make-believe zipper and to pull out her make-believe penis. Where to aim it, making sure not to splash outside the urinal was part two of the lesson. Try as she might she just couldn't keep all that black material of her habit high enough off the floor tiles without exposing her stockinged legs. At the same time, she was trying to not get her habit wet or touch the inside of the urinal. Her quest to maintain as much modesty as possible and to keep her habit clean and dry seemed more important to her than the art of properly demonstrating the use of this contraption called a urinal. She would grab onto one side of her voluminous habit and hitch it up to her waist so it wouldn't touch or contact the urinal, but as soon as she did that the other side would suddenly either give way and start to dangle dangerously close to it. She was so preoccupied in not showing the boys her petticoat and stockinged legs, she soon realized her on-the-spot tutorial was more daunting than she expected. Things were not going to her plan.

As this spectacle was unfolding, my mind wandered, and I asked myself 'how do they know how little boys pee in the first place'? 'Have they ever seen a little boy's penis before'? She certainly wasn't about to call it by its real name either. Her name for penis was "it."

"Take it out! Take it out from your underpants now!" she would screech. "Make sure you hold it inside the urinal, quickly do your business. It's a mortal sin to touch it so don't touch it too much or it will fall off!"

Oh great! One more thing to worry about while being in this place as my "it" was sure to fall off as I'm in the process of committing another mortal sin.

Mom used to call it my 'yang, yang'. That's what we called it at home and that's the only word I knew it by. When she said to take our "it" out, we wondered 'what's an it'? "Take your 'it' out, take it out" she kept barking. "Go to the urinal and do as I do!" she would order. The comical sight of her demonstration sent us all into fits of giggling. On hearing this she went into a blind rage. I could see her face turning bright red and the sweat was now beginning to form on her brow and staining her white wimple (the strange white material that framed her face). She suddenly grabbed an unsuspecting small boy, yanked his pants down and forcefully pulled his penis out with her fingers. Next, she pushed his face into the urinal as she was flushing it, drenching the terrified boy in water.

Her lesson for the day was now over and she stormed out through the door.

As this was taking place, I had learned a long time ago when to make myself scarce and to keep as quiet as a mouse. I would become as invisible as possible. Learning to hide, blend in or get away from a situation, which would later in life turn into an art form of survival. I was clever enough to know when the storm clouds were brewing in most situations to get away and get away fast! Sometimes it's a lot easier to blend into the background and become a total nobody. I was told once by a nun "Never ever draw attention to yourself as you're not worth looking at in the first place."

This became my unofficial motto. "Don't draw attention to yourself. Just blend in and keep quiet."

On one day during toilet training, all clothes were removed from girls and boys alike. I took myself off to the far corner of the bathroom and remember lying on my back on the floor tiles and feeling the unfamiliar warmth coming from underneath my naked body. It was never made clear why we had to undress on this occasion.

We simply followed another order.

However, laying there on the tiles, it was a blessing for me to feel the comforting warmth spreading over my naked backside (In contrast, the nuns always kept each of their classrooms unbearably cold, possibly for some penance or some twisted imaginary sin they, or we committed). As I was laying on my back staring up at the ceiling, daydreaming as children often do, suddenly a nun from another ward came up to me, stood over me and spread her legs wide open over my body. It happened quickly, catching me off guard, but I knew this was not a place to be. Did she know I was here? What do I do now? Should I make a sound to let her know I was down here? I took the option of not saying a word or moving a muscle - my newly adopted motto as I was terrified of getting a beating from her cane.

As I lay there motionless, I started to stare straight up her legs, looking at the inside of her habit, a dark and strange place which made me feel very uncomfortable. After a while my eyes started to adjust to the darkness of the inside of her black habit and I began to make out at first her black no-nonsense button-up boots, which led me to her ankle shrouded in her thick black stockings. Before I realized it, I was stunned to be now looking at the underpants she was wearing. As soon as my eyes finally adjusted to the darkness which enveloped me, I could suddenly see her under-panties, which to my astonishment were covered in tiny blue birds with yellow flowers around them and trimmed in frilly white lace.

She remained standing quite still over me for what I imagined was a very long time until I couldn't stand the heat inside her habit and it had become unbearable to breathe. I took the initiative and wiggled out as quietly as possible from under her skirt and crawled over to my designated corner hoping she hadn't noticed I was gone. As I scrambled to my corner she turned around and looked straight at me. I noticed a wry, sly smirk come across her face as if to say to me, "Did you get a good look? Did you see what I wanted you to see?" This was only done to me once and I made sure it would never be repeated.

From the safety of my vantage point in the corner, I was able to observe in stunned disbelief the full spectacle now unfolding in front of me. A scene of mass confusion with nuns running about and screaming at naked children, others whipping them with their trusty Rosary beads, rulers or canes, abusing and tormenting the smaller children who were not yet toilet trained and many still in nappies. Through the children's screams you could hear the nuns yell a tirade of abuse such as "You dirty disgusting girl, you're a filthy dirty boy. You brats clean this mess up if you know what's good for you. Now hurry it up!"

Our toilet lesson had ended for the day, only to start over again tomorrow, until we all got it right.

CHAPTER 8

MOMMY, WHAT'S A PERVERT?

9 am.-10 am.

For the one hour we had outside in the daylight it was a joy just to be as far away from the nuns as possible. Although there was precious little in the way of toys for us to play with, it didn't matter much to me. To the nuns' way of thinking they did not believe children should be wasting time in the pursuit of playing frivolous games and enjoyment.

I didn't care what they thought of us.

We had one hour of blissful freedom. Fortunately for us it was the only time the nuns never came outdoors, so we had a mistaken belief that we could do pretty much as we pleased with the limited time and toys. I do remember the school having one swing set, one skipping rope and one slide for over one hundred children to play on. Not much, but we didn't care. Talking was frowned upon as an instrument of the devil, I spent most of my time sitting around and pretending to be my hero the cowboy, Roy Rogers, and playing with my imaginary galloping painted pony, Trigger.

For me it was a time of peace and quiet.

Anything that would keep me away from the nuns was play time. It was a time for me to go into my quiet corner of the yard and pretend to be somebody, anybody or anything that would transport me away from this hellhole that was called a school.

One day Miss Gordon, a lay person, who was the housekeeper at the school, caught me playing Doctors and Nurses with one of the schoolgirls. It was innocent enough and we were only showing our body parts to one another, trying to figure out why we were so different 'down below.' After all it wasn't much different than us being naked during our toilet training now was it? Miss Gordon's job description was Head Housekeeper to the nuns and Playground Supervisor. Since the nuns rarely ventured into the playground her main duty was to supervise us and to report any goings-on to Mother Superior.

And report back she did.

Before any of us knew what was happening, I saw the Mother Superior running out her door like the devil himself was after her and making a bee line straight towards us. She ran up to the girl I was playing with and proceeded to slap her across the face so hard it sent her flying across the bitumen. She screamed at her,

"You're a filthy, dirty little whore."

Next, she swung around at me and with both hands grabbed me hard around the neck to choke me as she dragged me across the yard, beating me ferociously across my head with her hand, leading me to her upstairs office. She threw me into her office, slammed the door behind us and as she spun around, I noticed that part of her habit had become tangled up and stuck inside her shoe. She caught me taking a quick look at her slightly exposed stockinged ankle and in a blind rage started to beat me with her ruler across my bare knuckles while screaming that I was a,

"Disgusting little pervert."

Most of the times the nuns tried not to leave any tell-tale marks on our bodies by targeting areas that were covered by clothing.

"I'm telling my Mommy on you" I cried, as I cowered in the corner. I wasn't going to let her get away with it this time. "You're going to get into big trouble," I sobbed. "You'll see. My Mommy is going to be really mad at you."

I was determined to tell Mom what they had done to us, but the nuns were not only crafty but clever and very resourceful. They would always get to the parents first with an air-tight alibi. Mother Superior stated to my mother, in her now all-too strange and sweet angelic voice, that I had either fallen off a swing or I was fighting with another boy in the playground. She slowly turned to me and placed her cold hands on my cheeks and with a threatening stare hissed "Poor little boy. But boys will be boys, now won't they?" This exchange told me I had better keep my mouth shut if I knew what was good for me.

I was beaten and couldn't win. We were all beaten.

No one listened to us, no one took our complaints seriously. Why would they? We were just children and we only imagined the things that went on. Mom often would tell me I was telling tales, exaggerating or at worse telling a lie. She would say things like "Nuns wouldn't do things like that honey, so stop this lying once and for all."

So, it was useless for any of us to complain. They had won once again. By the time we got home I did manage to ask my Mom

"Mommy, what's a pervert?"

CHAPTER 9

GOD, I NEED A CIGARETTE!

11am.-12am.

This was our enforced nap-time whether we were tired or not. By now we understood that when an order was given by the nuns to go and sleep it was to be obeyed at all costs.

All one hundred and fifty of us were marched into another unusually cold part of the convent called the dormitory. Each of us had our own small bed to sleep in which had a number on it that we had to remember. I used to write my special number on the inside of my hand and just match up the number to the bed assigned to me. Some children had great difficulty in remembering their number being only four or five years of age. On each cot was placed one pillow and one scratchy and thin blanket. Once we had located our beds, we had to stand by them and await further instruction. Next, Mother Superior would come in and thump her cane on the hardwood floors which was her command for us to kneel by our cots and recite the Lord's Prayer completely before we could think of getting off that cold floor.

Once in our cots, we were ordered to keep our mouths shut, to keep all body parts covered, with absolutely no arms or legs protruding out from the blankets. All the time various nuns would be saying loudly "Do not wet your cot! Do not speak! Do not move and if you do you will be taken out to be severely whipped and go without lunch!" I would always pretend to be asleep when the nuns came around to do their checking on us. I couldn't understand why they had to constantly check on us all the time. What possible trouble could we do or get into anyway?

Most of the time I wasn't the least bit sleepy and preferred to keep my eyes closed when they walked by yet always stay alert and on my guard. However, today was different and I found myself drifting blissfully into a deep sleep. On this day, whilst asleep, I accidentally let my arm and hand slip out from under my blanket. As soon as this occurred a nun descended on me like a vulture coming in for a feed. Her screaming alone woke me and everyone else up with a sudden jolt. She came up to me and slammed her swinging chained crucifix hard down onto my hand with a sickening thud. I remember crying out in agony and terror. Blood now was falling onto the floor fuelling the nun's rage.

"Boy! Did I not tell you no arms or legs out from under your blanket! Why do you constantly disobey me?"

As I was sobbing and saying, "I'm sorry sister, I didn't mean it sister," she pulled me from my cot, forcing me on my hands and knees, and made me scrub my blood from the floor. As I was doing this, I inadvertently overheard this nun say to another,

"God, I need a cigarette to calm my nerves. Take over sister" and out the door she flounced without a care or concern in the world. It was as if nothing had happened.

Some of us from time to time were dragged from our slumber for the slightest misdemeanour apparently committed whilst asleep. Most of us never knew why we were being punished in the first place. We never ever saw anything coming. As we kept our eyes firmly shut, we could hear some of the children who were dragged from their cots say,

"I'm sorry sister. I didn't mean it sister. But I didn't do anything sister."

Questioning was useless. Crying for your Mommy was a waste of time.

Most of the time we never slept for fear of any more repeats. We were all too frightened to move and just laid there pretending to be asleep. I finally learned it would be safer to keep awake with one eye opened, my wits about me and my ears finely tuned. Fear is a powerful force to reckon with when you're very young and vulnerable with no-one to call on for help.

It can affect one's personality and destroy your spirit.

CHAPTER 10

THE LUNATICS ARE IN CHARGE

12 midday-3 pm.

After lunch we received religious instruction for the salvation of our wicked souls. For children of our age of only four and five it was an unbearably boring time of day. How we could possibly understand, much less read, the Bible was anyone's guess. And so, we sat perfectly still, listening to the nuns droned on and on for three hours about our sins and that of mankind. It was pure torture for us all. They said strange words like 'thee' and 'thou' and we wondered what they were talking about. Questions weren't tolerated, as asking them would deem you to be a troublemaker. All the time I couldn't stop thinking what sins we could have possibly committed in the first place.

What about the sins of the nuns? Does God know about them? Does he know what they get up to?

I didn't think he cared much anyway.

Since we were all too young to be able to read or write we were ordered to recite everything that was spoken to us by the nuns with no mistakes or deviations whatsoever. It didn't matter if we never understood what was being said or barked at us, we just had to look interested and not to ask any questions. It was important to nod enough to look like you're paying attention, or in other words, lie.

If we were not loud enough with our correct answers, showed enough reverence, or had the appropriate answers to their questions, then you were promptly dragged out of the classroom into the hallway or any convenient place and whipped by the nuns with their dreaded Rosary beads or cracked over the head with their ruler. We often would sit at our desks and hear screams coming from the hallway or from other classrooms which could only mean one thing; someone was getting the hell beaten out of them. You would shake in your seat wondering where the screaming was coming from and who was the latest victim.

You would thank your lucky stars it wasn't you.

Not this time anyway.

Looking back, the school now reminds me more of an asylum for lunatics, except we knew then, as now, we weren't the crazy ones. The nuns were the lunatics and they were firmly in charge.

CHAPTER 11

AND THE OSCAR GOES TO...

3 pm.

As we sat in the classroom, being told once again we were all wicked and evil children, your eyes would wander to peek at the clock on our classroom wall, wishing it would go faster. I couldn't tell time, no one could, but I knew when the big hand was on the twelve and the little hand was on the three, Mom would be waiting for me outside of the gates and her all-too familiar scent of cigarettes and coffee would greet me in a warm embrace. At last that glorious hour of 3 pm. arrived. The bell would finally ring for us to be released from this hellhole. By this stage I didn't give a damn what the old dragons from hell were mumbling on about. It didn't matter as I was going home with my Mom and far away from this madhouse, they called a school.

And that's something they could never take away from me, my Mom.

As we were once again being herded into an assembly line to wait for our mothers to come through the iron gates, the nuns would nervously walk up and down, primping and preening us as if we were their prized pets about to go on show. Some of the nuns looked genuinely nervous. Would the parents notice anything amiss? Would some of the parents ask embarrassing questions about certain tell-tale marks or bruising? Would a child dare speak out against us once they got home? I'm sure they all must have thought about this one time or another. But in no way did it ever moderate their anger or treatment towards us. However, then it dawned on me why they were making such a fuss over us, now as we were about to go home. They wanted us to look our best so they would look good too. It was all an 'act' of 'caring.'

And what an Academy Award performance they put on for the parents. Even the dreaded Mother Superior was putting on a show of smiles. She seemed to almost radiate a certain glow as if she had just won the Academy Award for Best Actress.

I was understandably surprised they could do it so well and with so much conviction. It was now frustratingly useless to complain as they would only deny it or make up a story to cover themselves. With their faces of angelic serenity, who would believe our stories anyway? What artists they were, bravo! No parent in their right mind would question a nun and who would dare to anyway, not unless she wanted her child to be expelled? The nuns knew that power and fear kept them safe and immune from questions.

They were clever, I will give them that.

As our Moms arrived that afternoon one nun came up to my mother and pulled her away from me and said to her in the sweetest voice, I had ever heard come out of her mouth

"Your son Madam exhibits signs of a wickedness and has a stubborn streak in him that will surely be his ruin if not corrected at once. We, of course, are all too happy to help him overcome this."

Strange I thought as only minutes before she was jackbooting her way up and down the line of children, hissing and spitting her venomous warnings at us about our daily sins and that we will eventually be on "a one-way road trip to hell." Then you would hear the sweet voices coming from them in perfect unison

"We will see you all tomorrow morning children, bright and early my dears, be good now and don't forget to say your prayers."

What parent could possibly think otherwise but goodness and virtue coming from these sweet ladies? What the nuns meant to say to us was if we talked, they would be waiting for us the next day. I often wondered if some of the parents did know what was going on in that convent. Some probably did, others, I'm sure, chose deliberately not to think or speak about the horrid possibilities. Whether you knew, suspected or not, no-one dared to speak out or complain about the various odd marks or welts on our bodies. Would things have changed back then if someone did speak out? I doubt it as it was the 1950's and the parents who were so poor and desperate knew they had to also keep their mouths shut and just to play along was the safest option. They were so grateful that someone as 'good' as the nuns would look after their child and do it for free. After all the marks and bruises did come from playing on the school grounds didn't, they?

The nuns said so and they wouldn't lie anyway, would they?

CHAPTER 12

FREEDOM

Age five, November 1955

This was a good year and a good day for me as it ended my 'indentured servitude' and misery to the women that called themselves the Brides of Christ. I went in not quite a four-year-old, totally innocent of the ways of the church and was now leaving at five with a loathing and bitterness not often found in a child of that tender age. I detested the Catholic Institution then as I do now with its teachings, nuns, priests and rich trappings that invariably seem to keep the poor in blissful ignorance. I hated them for what they did to all of us, including making us scrub the floors on our hands and knees, the constant cleaning of their toilets, the never-ending prayers, cowing to their every whim and the all too familiar beatings.

To this day I firmly believe they still turned a blind eye to what occurred back then and what, must still be going on in other institutions today, around the world. Not only in the U.S but now countries such as Ireland, Canada and Australia are all being brought into the spotlight by children who are now adults. Unfortunately, the Catholic Church has very deep pockets. You can ask your questions, but you'll be lucky to get an answer.

Well an honest one from them anyway.

We were constantly being brow-beaten by the nun's golden rule that "Silence was Golden" but to us it meant only one thing, intimidation and keep your mouth shut. The education they gave us was entirely based on fear, brutality and intimidation,

What I base all religion on today.

I was once told that more people have died in the name of religion than all the other major wars throughout history.

Finally, the sweet day came when we were led out from our classrooms and told to wait patiently for our parents behind those dreaded iron gates. The nuns had such sweet smiles and loving, innocent faces. I couldn't believe or understand why, after a year of hell in this place, none of us ever saw this kind of behaviour on display. Who did they think they were kidding anyway? Not me that's for sure. Maybe the parents were fooled but certainly not us who were leaving this wretched hell of a place. I couldn't help but notice some of them laughing with a puffed-up pride in themselves that they single-handedly instilled good Roman Catholic virtues into these poor wretches. Their work was done, and they looked so smug and confident that they had done such a good job on us. Indeed, they believed this as they were confidently sending us out into the world better people than when we first shuffled through those iron gates a year ago. I couldn't help but feel sadness for the younger children that had to endure another year of hell and the new ones about to enrol.

As we were leaving, I turned, just as the gates slammed closed behind us, knowing my time had at last come and I was now safe and free and in the hands of my Mom. I broke away from Mom's grasp and ran back to the closed gates and in a voice, I didn't know I had, screamed out at the top of my lungs what I thought of them but was always too afraid to say,

"You're all very bad, bad people and you're the bad ones not us that's going to hell and I will never forget what you did to us. I hate you; I hate all of you and hope you all die and burn in your hell. I will tell on all of you."

The wretched nun who always let us in the mornings recoiled in abject horror and disbelief that someone would dare raise a voice against them. As soon as Mom heard my outburst she gasped and jerked my hand as we hurriedly walked down the pathway towards home. She never asked why I said these things and we never spoke of it again. But I'm sure she knew; they all must have known something terribly wrong was going on at The Immaculata convent. Maybe they were as intimidated by the nuns as we were to speak out. But not me.

My name is Greg and I will never be quiet again.

To my utter horror and disbelief a few years later I found out I had to go through one more Christian rite of passage with the Catholic Church. This was to be my first Holy Communion. My mother was so excited and proud of the fact that I would be the very first child on her side of the family to take Holy Communion. To see the look of pride that her son was finally getting this blessed sacrament from the Catholic Church sent chills up and down my spine once again. I knew it was such an important event for her, however I did not share her enthusiasm. I decided to go through this charade only for Mom's sake as it meant so much to her. However, at the last minute I was mysteriously denied this most sacred ritual that all good Catholic children must go through. At the final hour before the ceremony began, we were told by the very same priest who hated me for daring to question him about Adam and Eve, that I wasn't a good enough candidate to go through this ceremony due to any number of excuses he had mysteriously conjured up.

He did finally say I was "not up to scratch" with reciting the Lord's Prayer. I protested that I could recite, write and do the Lord's Prayer backwards, standing on my head and all perfectly well, thank you. Try as I did to placate him by saying the Lord's Prayer, for some reason it was never good enough for him. He would always find some fault in my recital.

I wondered if there were other reasons why I failed to make my first communion. I was to find out years later the real reason.

One day Mom may have had one too many cocktails over evening dinner. She blurted out that she might have had a tiny something to do with me not going to my first communion. She continued that Father O'Brady, the very same despicable drunk of an Irish priest of my convent years, came to our door one afternoon and demanded from Mom the enormous sum of $500. This was an astronomical sum back in the 1950's. There was no way Mom could afford such a sum for the church. When asked why so much money was demanded he arrogantly stated that this was the money needed from her to pay penance for not going to church every Sunday and being a divorcee. We knew the real reason he wanted the money and extortion was not beneath him.

Mom was shocked but was more indignant than anything that here sat this pompous hypocrite who was perfectly happy to take her money when she could scrape it together for the Sunday collection plate. He was always happy to accept her cooking for church fetes, and back then it never bothered him that she was a divorced mother. Now suddenly, I was 'deemed' to be not 'worthy' enough a Catholic unless the sum stated was paid in full and only then gaining his assurances that I would be allowed to finish my First Holy Communion. It depended on the money and it had to be paid to him personally and promptly

"Cash please, no cheques thank you."

Now Mom, who was barely five-foot-tall in shoes, sprang off the couch quicker than a priest could say 'Amen.' With one hand she snatched the stunned priest by his coat collar and with the other hand grabbed him by the backside of his pants and promptly frog marched him to the front door, throwing him out the door with some timely expletives only Mom knew. His trusty Bible followed quickly having been thrown by Mom and with deadly aim striking him on the head. He was last seen briskly walking down the street clutching his Rosary beads with Mom's curses ringing in his ears. He was never seen or heard from again.

No wonder I never took my First Communion; they were too scared of Mom.

Brava Mom!

CHAPTER 13

WHO'S YOUR DADDY

Early November, age six 1957

Being six years of age, I never truly understood, but found out later, that my mother was always very lonely and sad for most of her young adult life. She was the type of person who needed the security of a man to love and to be loved back.

Mom, it turns out, was a type of woman who thought she needed a man to make herself complete. She wanted that story of domestic bliss and happiness with a man like you saw on TV every night. Once again, she felt life was passing her by. I cried with her and wondered why I wasn't enough for her. I would put both my tiny arms around her neck and do my best to cradle her wet cheeks and say

"I can look after you Mommy so don't worry. You have me all to yourself so I will take good care of you so please don't cry anymore." Through her sob's Mom started to feel she wasn't good enough to find or keep a man.

The days she was sad, I would always tell her I would be rich one day and marry her and pay her bills and have lots and lots of money. That way she would never have to worry about anything ever again. I was determined not to fulfil the prophecy of the nuns that "one day I would cause my mother nothing but tears and sadness." A faint smile would come across her tear stained face as she held me close to her chest gently rocking me. As a young boy you think you are the centre of everyone's universe and especially your mother's. After all, your needs are the only thing that matter, aren't they?

It was early November 1957 and I'm still six years old.

It was one of those rare days when all seemed right with our world. My birthday would soon be here and for once we both were very happy. I was told by Mom that I had a big surprise waiting for me when I came home from school. It had to be one of two things. A new uncle was either on the horizon or I was finally getting my Roy Rogers cowboy hat. But for now, it was just the two of us and that's the way I liked it. Mom was unusually bubbly and giggling like a young schoolgirl. Whatever it was that was making Mom happy made me feel happy. With this new uncle coming over I figured at long last I might get this elusive Roy Rogers Cowboy Hat from him, something I had always wanted but never received from my previous uncles. It was a win, win situation as far as I was concerned.

It just couldn't get any more exciting for the both of us.

I raced home from school and since it was almost my seventh birthday the thought of presents and getting that coveted cowboy hat was too much for me to bear. I barged through the front door and scanned my surrounding area for my new hat that I was sure would be with my new uncle. I ran throughout the house looking from room to room for this surprise that Mom had promised. Not once did I notice the man sitting with Mom on the couch. Little did we know this same man would not only destroy my mother's life but nearly kill me.

Suddenly, in front of me was a hulk of a man with a dark ruddy complexion, embracing in a passionate kiss with Mom, when I inadvertently rushed in and broke the spell. He slowly turned to face me with a look of intense annoyance at being interrupted. His giant frame, slowly rose from the couch and said in a low sinister voice,

"Well boy, it looks like I'm going to have to make sure you don't do that anymore, now won't I. You need to be taught some manners."

His glare sent a cold shiver through me as I knew he meant business. Mom suddenly said "Honey come and say hello. He's your new daddy. His name is Larry. Can you call him daddy for me?"

She had inadvertently forgotten to mention they had just gotten married. This was a new word I had never heard of before, uncle yes but daddy no. I swore from that day onwards he would never hear me calling him by that name, daddy.

Then I heard: "Yeah, call me daddy why don't ya kid."

Children aren't stupid and often have a keen insight into what's going on around them that adults sometimes conveniently ignore. This insight unfortunately gets lost as we get older, but I knew right away this was a man not to be trifled with in any way. I politely said hello to Larry and consciously refused to call him daddy. Larry was the only name he'd get from me I thought. As my Mom left the room, she casually said

"You two boys play nice now and I'll be back in a jiffy."

Mom was back in the role of the dutiful housewife we both had seen on TV most nights. You know the type, apron over a beautiful dress and in high heels, hair perfectly coifed and preparing drinks for the two of them. Larry slowly brought his hulking dark frame down to my height and looked me straight in the eyes. As he stared at me, I instinctively took a step back. As I started to move, he grabbed me roughly by the hand and pulled me close to his face. Staring back at me through coal black eyes I could only see the eyes of a dead man. He smelled like the priest I once knew, full of cheap whisky and cigarettes but with another peculiar smell added to the mix. It was a sickly-sweet greasy smell that permeating the air around him. I came to recognise that smell was coming from his jet-black hair, slicked down with a hair cream called back then, Brylcream. In a low, deep and sinister voice so Mom would not be able to hear him, he said,

"Stay out of my way kid and we will get along just fine. If you don't do what I say around here, you're in for a whole lot of pain. You don't want me to hurt you now do you? Do you understand me?"

I stammered out a weak "Yes Larry" as my instincts told me to slowly back away, nodding in agreement yet not fully understanding what he meant.

Larry was born into a family of social outcasts and misfits to a woman who was probably certifiably insane. No-one knew who she was or where she originally came from. Larry never knew his real father and he was only allowed to call his mother by her first name of Doreen. He knew from a very early age never to call her 'mother' in public if he knew what was good for him. She ran with many aliases but settled for the name of Doreen as she thought it sounded glamorous and felt it suited her personality. That's what she told her many 'clients'. She figured the less they know about her the better and easier for her to cover her tracks.

There is no mistaking the fact that she was in her day a high-class hooker. Doreen was notoriously well known throughout the mid-western states of Kansas, Oklahoma and the Texas pan handle in the 1930's. For a brief time, she hooked up with the Barrow Gang better known as the famous Bonnie and Clyde, the bank robbers. I have seen many a happy picture of her with a machine gun in one hand and a pistol in the other while smoking a large cigar. She would have her daintily clad silk-stockinged leg seductively resting on the running board of a Packard automobile that was supposedly Clyde Barrow's getaway car. The car was used in numerous bank robberies throughout the south and mid-west. Bonnie would usually be the one taking the happy photos.

Whether Doreen was involved in any of these robberies we will never know for sure.

While she and Larry were constantly on the move across the mid-western states of America, she picked up numerous young gentlemen along the way to 'keep her company.' Doreen liked her men young, very young. Numerous times she would make love to them in the back seat of her car while the child Larry, seated in the front, had to pretend he didn't know what was going on. This was either a form of punishment or most likely it was to teach him a lesson. In her mind he was a useless mill stone around her neck and a constant burden to have around. Actual parental concerns for his moral character meant nothing to her. She simply had none in the first place. If Larry did complain or make himself known from the front seat, she would kick him out the car and make him sleep out on some dirty back road. She would drive off to finish her business transaction, later picking him up in the morning where she had dumped him the night before.

Larry suffered innumerable, constant humiliations at the hands of his mother. For example, she would always tell new friends and 'clients' that the child was the son of a friend of hers. She would make it known it was her Christian duty to take in the child and care for him. However, when it came time to conduct her business transactions he would be conveniently pushed into the background.

Little wonder that this boy would grow up into this hideous monster who now claimed to be my new father.

I maintain that you are not the product of your parents or upbringing as everyone has their own cross in life to carry. We must be able and strong enough to rise above it and not to make the same mistakes our parents did.

Some people would probably say that he wasn't really to blame for the pain he inflicted or caused others. He was the product of his environment and nurtured in this way, or so the experts would say. Where do we put the blame and where does the evil stop? Do we blame the mother for everything that happened to him and my family? Back in the thirties and forties I doubt there was a system in place to help him or his mother and there certainly wasn't much of a system in place to help us in the fifties and sixties.

When he finally did get his hands on us, it was too late for him and for us as well. The seed of brutality, evil and psychopathic behaviour had been passed on from the master to the apprentice, her son. There would be no turning back.

As the years rolled by Doreen was noticing that Larry was exhibiting more and more signs of becoming violently unhinged. There were times she felt she couldn't control him any longer to do her bidding. If anyone ever made the mistake of crossing her son he would snap and become extremely violent, lashing out at anyone in his immediate vicinity. He could no longer temper his numerous outbursts of rage and took a perverted pleasure in causing those around him the maximum suffering. Mental pain leaves no visible marks or bruising; not on the outside anyway.

If he couldn't' beat up people, he would do unspeakably cruel things to stray dogs or cats to satisfy his urges for pleasure.

Doreen eventually got rid of him by dumping him into a quasi-boy's brigade called the CC scouts who took in troubled youth and tried turning them into men. This only fuelled his instability and loathing for her even more. After years of being told what to do and when to do it, he was finally expelled from the CC's labelled a person too difficult to handle. He later tracked Doreen down and exacted a brutal revenge on her for the treatment he endured for the years he spent with her and in the CC camps. It was her time to pay the price for how his life turned out by beating her up so badly that she was not seen or heard from again for years. That was until she turned up unexpectedly one day to inspect Larry's new wife, Flo.

Mom was not only married to a madman but had to contend with a mother-in-law who hated the very breath she drew and spent the rest of her time making Mom's life a nightmare.

One month later against all odds, my brother Kenny came into the world.

Larry was married once before to a woman who was called, Nora, who saw his mean streak and packed her bags, taking her two kids, and moved straight in with her mother-in-law, Doreen. Nora became a close ally of hers and confidant.

Together they did everything to meddle in our lives. Doreen even once told Mom that she was nothing but a two-bit whore and would never be good enough for her son.

Maybe the acorn really doesn't fall far from the tree after all.

CHAPTER 14

GOING SOMEWHERE?

February 1958

I'm barely seven years old now and it's the first time I'm seeing this strange colour.

It is a peculiar shade of red that paralyses me and makes me gasp for air. My heart is pounding and yet time seems to have stopped. Only this colour of the red associated with rubies has this profound effect. I am filled with dread as it evokes dark memories I try to keep hidden away. I have an overwhelming urge to run but there is no place to go. All my senses are dulled, as though I am in a fog.

What is happening to me?

I will try to explain.

I find myself lying face down on the dining room floor of our home at Barnett Way. As I slowly began to push my head up from the floor, I couldn't understand how I got there. I suddenly became mesmerized at seeing a strange colour with a smell that I had never experienced before that was now flowing and closing in around me. I stared at it in utter astonishment as a tide of ruby red liquid crept around my head and face and cradled my body in its warm liquid embrace.

I struggled to pull my arms and hands up, turning them from side to side in total amazement to see they were also covered in this same sticky red fluid. At first, I couldn't think what it was or where it was coming from. How odd it looked as it slowly oozed past my head, thick, red and shiny as. It was strange how it moved across the hardwood floors, it filled all the cracks and imperfections of the floor where I lay. I had never seen this amount of blood before and couldn't comprehend where it was coming from. I wasn't even sure it was blood.

I felt no pain, there was no panic and no recollection of what had happened to me. Surely, I must be able to feel or hear something by now. I was strangely numb from my waist down. As all this was racing through my head, I couldn't help still wonder how rich in texture and colour this red liquid looked and that it was beautiful as it slowly made its way past my prone body.

My first instinct was that I had somehow made this mess and that I needed to clean it up quickly before 'he' gets home or there would be hell to pay. He liked his house clean and everything had to be in its right place. It was only when I managed to pull myself partially off the floor, I caught a glimpse of myself in the mirror and recoiled in utter horror to see looking back at me a strange and hideous creature with a fixed gaze of terror on its face. Oh, my God, who is this monster staring back at me? It was me! Suddenly I realised that all this red stuff that was all over the walls, floor and furniture was blood, and it was coming from me.

There was so much blood I had difficulty figuring out exactly where it was coming from. I remember looking in the mirror that my eyes were now black and blue and strangely filled with blood. That's the last thing I remember seeing before I Momentarily lapsed into unconsciousness.

Mom's once white and clean walls that she took pride in were now splattered and smeared everywhere in this ruby-red coloured mess. When I woke up again, I could see a bloody pattern splattered onto the walls in the shape of a beautiful necklace. Red handprints covered the walls as if a child had been busy finger painting all over them.

In stunned bewilderment I noticed that no surface was spared from the carnage. Curtains, furniture and Mom's once clean house was now stained throughout with ruby red droplets.

"What's going on?", I finally screamed out. "Mama, where are you? Help me!"

Was this bloody mess mine, I wondered? As I looked at the bloody walls it slowly dawned on me that it must be all mine. I had hoped it was coming from somebody else. But why from me?

Suddenly, I could hear my Mom screaming out in panic "Run honey, run! Get out! Get away from here, now!" But where to? I tried to get off the floor to escape this chaos but found my legs would not work.

I tried several times to get to my feet only to find myself crashing back down onto the floor screaming in agony. Next, I tried crawling to get into the adjoining room, but intense pain prevented me from moving at all.

Despite my injuries, I was gripped by an overpowering need to get away as fast as possible. With all my strength I started to drag myself with my arms as best as I could along the floor. I was not sure where I was going to or what exactly I was trying to get away from. As I moved, I noticed the strange squelching sounds that my body was making inching my way along the hallway.

Suddenly, I immediately realised I was being dragged backwards, slowly at first, then with a violent jolt.

Wild panic now set in as I tried to use my arms and hands in a swimming fashion in a desperate bid to stop being pulled backwards against my will. Slamming my arms down I cried in agony in a futile attempt to resist this invisible force.

By now the blood on the floor was no longer pooled around me and I suddenly realized it was being smeared and left behind on the floor as my limp body was now being dragged through it. I turned to see what was happening and I suddenly realised it was 'him.' Larry had a firm hold of me and I could just make out the expression on his face that had now turned into a hideous demonic mask. Sweat and blood dripped from his face as he flicked his head back and forth to remove it from his eyes. He laughed and said, "Going somewhere?" he smiled as he gripped tighter to my broken legs.

Utter panic took a hold of me.

I screamed, "Leave me alone! Get away from me!" But nothing I did could stop him from dragging me back into the kitchen where it all began.

It turned out that the monster had been hiding behind the kitchen door of Barnett Way and was now on the loose and on a rampage. Struggling was useless. He had me and wasn't about to let me go.

Not this time, not ever.

(Little did I realise that both my legs had been broken, some of my ribs were cracked and my nose was broken. The reason I kept blacking out all the time and going into unconsciousness was due to a fractured skull).

I was eventually taken away by ambulance to the Mercy Hospital where it took me two months of recovery before I could go back to school. Funny, no charges were ever brought against Larry. We both knew what would happen if we did.

"You better keep your fuckin traps shut if you know what's good for you!"

CHAPTER 15

DINNER TIME

6 pm. Sharp!

Dinner was one of the few times for me to see my Mom as time for any interactions outside my bedroom was shrinking fast. With Mom working fulltime and Larry imposing more restrictions on both of us, I began to feel invisible as I was slowly being marginalized from my mother's influence, like I was being slowly erased.

For the average normal family having dinner together is a time to exchange polite conversation, enjoy a good meal cooked by Mom and generally feel relaxed. This was never the case at our house, instead it was always a time of great stress. Mom especially felt this as though her cooking skills were always put to the test by Larry.

She would sustain several brutal beatings from him regarding his meal if it wasn't done in the way he ordered. She would be ordered what he wanted everyone to eat, and how it was to be prepared. There would always be something wrong with what or how she cooked any of her meals. One night just before dinner was to be served, my brother and I noticed Mom had two massive black eyes for something Larry perceived she had done incorrectly. With her eyes swollen and almost shut, that night's dinner was fraught with extreme tension.

The poor woman literally shook with fear at mealtime. In fact, we all did. Mom was expected as usual to continue doing what a good and obedient housewife does best, cook and keep her mouth shut.

One night my brother and I were called for dinner and we eased into our chairs not wishing to draw any more attention to ourselves. I'm not sure what we hoped to accomplish by being as discreet as possible, invisibility would have been nice. This night he turned and locked his all too familiar cold eyes on me. He had me dead in his sights for something, but for what, I had no idea.

Larry always sat in front of me, Mom sat to my right and my little brother on the left. We were never allowed to look up from our plates, and most importantly never to look at him or anyone for that matter for the duration of the evening meal. Speaking was absolutely forbidden. He had stated that tonight no one would be allowed to talk at the dinner table "from now on."

He would be the only one to ask the questions and we were expected to answer quickly and appropriately. End of story.

It was always so difficult and exhausting to know how to act as he continued to enforce countless regulations. For example, dinner must be on the table at six pm. If Mom was late for any reason, the food she had prepared would then be dumped into the garbage and we all went hungry.

For me it was becoming increasingly difficult just to remember and keep all his numerous edicts straight. We were always in a constant state of confusion or agitation as orders were changed without notice to satisfy his sudden whims. One day we would be allowed to do this at the dinner table, the next it mysteriously changed, and we would be slapped or punched repeatedly across the face for not remembering the changes. Our dinner was more an ordeal of intimidation and fear than a process of eating. We expected the unexpected and always got the worse from him at dinner time.

He never disappointed us.

As he had ordered some time ago, we always had to eat virtually the same thing night after night, a piece of meat and two vegetables. The meat was always the cheapest cut because that's all Mom could afford. A glass of water was only to be served after dinner and, if lucky, dessert was always a glutinous tapioca pudding. No more no less. Mom was never allowed to cook or do anything different because that's what he liked so that's what we had to eat. His meat had to be cooked red raw and bloody. The bloodier the better with strict instructions that his meat be cooked for only a few seconds on each side with all the fat was to be left on. If it was good enough for him then it was good enough for all of us to eat the same way.

Then one-night Mom accidentally overcooked his steak by a few seconds longer than he liked. He took one mouthful and spat it into her face. He screamed at Mom "You're a useless fucking bitch who can't cook a decent fucking steak. What the hell's wrong with you Florence?"

The uneasy truce was now over.

As he picked his steak up and squeezed it in his tightly clasped fist, I could see the blood from it dripping down his arm and onto the table. He picked his plate up and hurled it against the wall behind me, missing me by inches, while all the time screaming at Mom to go and cook him "another fucking steak" and if she knew what was good for her, she had "better do it right this time or else." Mom quickly ran out the door, not to escape him, but to get to the butchers to buy him another steak.

We were shaking with fear waiting for Mom to get home, but we knew better than to say or do anything. Just stare down into your plate, don't move and don't make a sound, just wait. We would never dare take the initiative to move a muscle if you wanted to survive a dinner with him. Most humans would run away in abject terror, but it became our natural defence mechanism for us to stay completely still and say nothing. It was like being an animal caught in a car's headlights, momentarily paralysed with fear. I hated all foods that he liked that were served to us. Once he learned this, he got the greatest enjoyment seeing us squirm when his favourites like offal and rare and bloody steak was placed in front of us. It was 'his treat' for us, and a sly smirk would crawl across his face as Mom would nervously serve this meal knowing we hated it. Again, we knew it was going to be a bad night for us.

On another occasion, while he was out of the kitchen, he had previously ordered Mom to cook him rare liver and onions for dinner and as she was doing so, I whispered to her to please give me the smallest piece possible. She whispered to me, "Honey, I'll do my best, but it's going to be difficult, but I'll see what I can do." Larry was listening to our conversation from behind the kitchen door and heard everything. He knew what was going on between Mom and me and as we sat down for dinner, he promptly switched his plate with mine. I had now in front of me the largest, grey and rare piece of liver with its blood oozing from it and running off the plate. Larry sat there with that familiar smirk spread across his face and said to me "Thought you both were going to get away with it, didn't you? Now you're going to eat every bit of it, or I will personally shove it down your fucking throat."

Try as I might to eat even the smallest piece of the almost raw liver, I would always end up gagging on it and spitting it out onto my plate. He earlier forbade us to drink any water during mealtime until everything was consumed. I had no way of washing the putrid liver down or to mask the taste of it. He sat there laughing and smiling in his own sadistic way, enjoying the show unfolding in front of him. He stated I would not be leaving the table until every bit of the liver was consumed.

I stayed at the table for four hours crying and pleading with him not to make me eat any more. Each time I started to cry he would lean over the table, grab my head and slam my face down onto the plate and into the remaining liver. Then with his hands he would forcibly wrench my mouth open, take the liver and force feed me with his large, fleshy fingers. He would then smear the liver over my face as he pushed it further down my throat faster than I could chew or swallow. I gagged and vomited repeatedly, whereby he would merely fish through the remains with his fingers and continue his quest of force feeding me. Mom was totally powerless to do anything as she meekly sat with her head buried in her hands, looking at her own plate not saying a word.

Finally, in a very weak voice she said, "Please daddy, no more." Without missing a beat, he punched her in the face with his left hand sending her crashing onto the floor. She slowly picked herself up as if nothing had happened and staggered to the bathroom to get cleaned up. Her protest was useless, and it was over as far as he was concerned.

I knew in the end I would lose the battle and would wake up the next day to find he had placed the bloody liver and onions into a bowl and that it would be waiting for me in the morning for breakfast. It never occurred to me that Mom's and my blood was also mixed up with the liver as he had beaten me until I blacked out. I sat at the breakfast table the next morning, naked and crying and I forced the putrid meat into my mouth trying not to gag and vomit it all up again. He sat at the table in front of me smirking and laughing through the whole performance. Larry must have thought this was the funniest bit of entertainment he's seen in a long time.

CHAPTER 16

BARNETT WAY

Over the years my memory was made up by a constant nervous anxiety about being moved from one rented house to another. We never seemed to stay long enough to even settle into a house, much less a school. I never truly unpacked my small number of belongings and when it was time to move on again, I just closed my suitcase and figured well here we go again, thinking it would be like all the other times. It was just another temporary place until we could find something cheaper to move into. Then we would re-start our lives until Larry decided we needed to move. Every time we would relocate, Larry was always in a state of nervous tension, constantly looking out for something or someone. He could single-handily pack up an entire house in a matter of hours. Everything was thrown into boxes or haphazardly put into the back of a truck. He didn't care what got broken or what was left. If it was too big or not important to him it would invariably be left out on the street for anybody to collect. We tended to leave a lot of things behind in our many hasty moves. We never had a say in why we were always moving, and we never dared to ask him. I suspected, as we always moved in the middle of the night, it had something to do with un-paid rent. So here we were again, freezing in the depths of a winter's night, driving a broken-down old truck and moving to our new rental accommodation we would try to call home. For how long, would be anybody's guess.

As we drove up to the new house on Barnett Way, my first impression was that it was something right out of a gothic horror movie. Both Mom and I took an instant disliking to the house but for obvious reasons we kept that to ourselves and said nothing to Larry. There was something strange and eerie about this place.

At once, you were struck by how old the house was compared to the others on the block. It was the only house on the block that hadn't been renovated. The age of the house wasn't the only factor making it appear odd. It was grey and to my eight-year-old eyes had all the appearances of a haunted house.

To me the house just wanted to be left alone and empty.

Larry was told by the rental agency that the house was built in a neo-Spanish style which was typical of many Californian homes of the 1920's era. The front and back yards were quite big. There was a very large basement that had a peculiar smell wafting from it when you walked past. It became stronger when the heavy wooden cyclone doors were opened. The agent emphasised that the cellar was off limits to the tenants - making some flimsy excuse about the dirt, rats, spiders and an old oil heater. I needed no more convincing, but right away Larry's interest was piqued.

Funny, I thought, no mention of why it smelled so bad.

The rent was cheap and as far as Larry was concerned it was a done deal for him which meant none of us had any further say in the matter. If you looked at the house face on you could be mistaken in thinking the architect was quite mad in designing the house. The front had a centre upper balcony that overlooked the front steps and yard. The yard was enclosed by a four-foot-high wall that was removed soon after we moved in. To gain access to this yard one had to fight with a rusty metal gate that had a mind of its own. Often, we just scrambled over the wall as opposed to trying to fight opening the gate.

Another oddity was the two large windows facing the street. On the outside of these windows and bolted over each of them was a massive iron bar. Attached to the bar were heavy, grey curtains that were next to impossible to pull across by hand. Mom asked the landlord why they were so heavy and was told they were lined with a thin layer of lead. He had explained they were something to do with Russians and the atomic bomb. Why would anyone go to that trouble when there was a perfectly adequate basement, I thought? Pulling these exterior curtains across the windows was difficult for Mom due to their weight. When fully closed, light was completely obliterated. Mom once wondered aloud why anyone would go to all that trouble keeping light out. I casually said, "Or from anyone looking in?"

When Mom and I walked around to the back of the house, and I was still tightly clutching Mom's hand, we noticed a tiny sign over the basement door that read 'The Hiding Place.' Next morning the sign had mysteriously disappeared. It was an odd name I thought and wondered who or what would want to hide down there. I was certainly in no hurry to find out.

All these oddities only excited Larry even more. You never dared tell Larry what to do or not do. When the agent advised him that the basement was out of bounds, this became too much of a temptation to Larry. It was an irresistible challenge. He promptly took himself down the stairs and into the darkened basement to investigate things for himself. As he descended, he immediately noticed spaced around the basement six large mounds that looked like freshly dug graves. The strong foul odour did not seem to bother him.

Mom tried saying all kinds of positive things to me about the house to reassure Kenny and me. She was trying to take our minds off all the negative things we were thinking, noticing and feeling.

Upon entering the house, you noticed right away how bitterly cold it was inside with the smell of damp permeating everywhere. In future we found out no amount of heat from that ancient boiler in the basement would bring any warmth or comfort. The house floors were made of polished faded timber that creaked and groaned whenever someone walked over them. At times, late at night, you would swear that someone was walking around the house. Mom would always reassure us it was just the floorboards creaking by expanding and contracting throughout the night (Little did she realise but the creaking floor boards were often due to Larry roaming around the house from room to room with his gun, cocked and ready to fire at his imaginary intruders. In time those creaking floorboards would alert me and save me on numerous occasions).

The rent papers were quickly signed and that was the end of any potential discussions about our new home. I asked Mom many years later why she hated that house so much. She replied that the house seemed evil and came alive when Larry was in it. She would slowly trail off with words like, "Evil does bad things to people." She was dead right!

It was the beginning of our end.

Larry got his way. He got his house, and this is where we were going to stay. If we didn't like it, we could sleep down in the basement for all he cared. He constantly reminded me that since I came with Mom and she was his wife then I had no say in the matter. However, Larry would be heard saying even he hated the house and he often found excuses to keep away as much as possible. Suits me I thought. For the time being I prayed he would take his own advice and do just that, stay away and leave us in peace.

Walking by the cyclone doors to the basement I always shuddered at the smell coming from there. You couldn't help but quickly walk by. The doors were never secured and so would shake from the wind blowing through them. I always imagined that sound was someone was trying to escape from down there.

Throughout his ever-increasing screaming fits and violent rages Larry repeatedly warned us never to go down into the basement as "His things" were now being stored down there. Fine with me I thought as I had absolutely no desire to go down there in the first place. One night he suddenly ordered me into the basement under the pretext of getting more firewood for the fireplace as this was now our only means of heating. As I struggled opening the heavy cyclone doors my heart was pounding and I broke out in a cold sweat wondering what would be waiting for me. From the top near the doors all you could see were stairs descending into an unlit, steep black hole. Larry told me there was a hanging light bulb that I would be able to turn on once down there. Slowly I edged my way down the steps, groping the wall as I fumbled my way in the dark. Once I got to the half-way mark, I thought, what happens when I finally get to the bottom? Where do I go then? Where was the firewood located? And where was this hanging light bulb supposed to be?

The lower I descended the darker it became. Finally, I reached the bottom step. I tapped the floor gently with one foot to make sure I was at last on solid ground. By now I had absolutely no idea where the light bulb was located or which way to go to find it. Creeping my way slowly into the darkness, I realised I needed to find this elusive light bulb that was supposed to be dangling somewhere overhead. I stumbled around, waving my arms about in the darkness to try and find the light bulb. When at last I grabbed hold of it, to my horror I discovered it was indeed the light, but the globe had been removed. He had sent me down into a darkened basement knowing all the time there was no globe. As I realized what was going on Larry suddenly slammed the doors closed behind me, snapping his new padlock in place. To add to his amusement, he found it hilarious to start banging on the doors saying,

"You like it down their sissy boy? Have fun."

I stumbled through the darkness trying to feel my way in the direction for the stone steps. Climbing frantically to the top I reached the underside of the basement doors and banged hysterically on them. I struggled to lift the heavy door upwards. I was crying and begged him to let me out. All I heard was his laughing and the creaking floorboards above me as he paced around the house like the demented animal. He made me stay down there for hours as I groped blindly around the dirt floor trying to find a wall I could at least lean against. I sat in the dirt for hours shivering from the cold with my imaginary ghosts that kept me company. He only let me out when he grew tired of the joke.

Another example of his cruelty was to drag me to a tiny room contained inside the garage. Strange I thought, who would ever want to live in such a tiny room no bigger than a closet. It was in a filthy state as decades of garbage had collected inside as well as out. The garbage outside the tiny room seemed to move and heave from all the rats, spiders and snakes crawling underneath it as they tried desperately to avoid being a meal in the garage food chain. In my mind I knew all I had to do was walk across the garbage to get out. Yet I was petrified with fear and frozen to this spot. This was one room he didn't need a lock.

Another favourite pastime of Larry's was to plant dead spiders throughout my bedroom. He knew I was terrified of spiders and when I was at school, he would hide them in my bed, my shoes, my clothes and I even found some pressed in between the pages of my schoolbooks. At night and with great trepidation I would give my room a thorough inspection before I would even think of getting into bed. I'd scan the entire floor looking under the bed, inside my shoes and finally throwing the bed sheets and blankets off the bed before I got in. As expected, there would always be a 'present' waiting for me. Too often I would find either a large black spider or a cockroach tucked under my pillow or at the bottom of my bed. When he had finished his little fun, I could hear his high pitch squeal of delight and giggling like a little child each time I screamed after discovering one of his hidden creatures. Then I knew his fun was over and I might finally get some sleep.

There were only two bedrooms inside the house, and I was beginning to worry Larry might have plans for me to stay in that tiny room inside the garage. He kept saying it would make a great bedroom for someone, someone that needed a backbone, meaning me. I knew at once I was slowly being marginalized from the family. Luckily, he moved his boat into the garage and that small room was no longer an option. My two-year-old brother, and I finally got to share the second small bedroom inside the house.

This room had one rather large window overlooking the backyard and garbage bins. I would lie petrified and motionless in bed glancing at the window wondering what sick and twisted games he would play next.

It always started well after midnight. I would wait for the familiar sounds and then track in my mind the course he would take in his journey to my bedroom window. Initially there were the familiar 'clicks' of his bedroom door when he quietly opened and closed it. I knew then he would be making his way stealthily out through the back door and into the backyard. Next came his footsteps as he moved slowly across the yard. At times, a sudden crackling of leaves or maybe a snapped twig would signal he was not far away. I silently lay there plotting his course across the yard to the point where the rustling of the camellia bush, adjacent to our bedroom, meant that he had finally arrived and was looking at us through the window.

Larry liked to stand outside the bedroom window at night either in his underwear or naked, just looking at me while I pretended to be asleep. I always froze with fear and never moved a muscle, but I knew he was there. Sometimes he would watch me at night when I was getting undressed for bed, he would stand there staring. At other times he would lean against our bedroom door, gently turn the doorknob to see if I had locked it and listen to any sounds, he might hear coming from us.

Some nights I could sense he was standing next to my bed just staring down at me as I pretended to sleep. Mostly he would get his pleasure being outside looking through any window of the house, so long as he got a view of me. I knew he was out there, but nothing was ever said as it was safer to keep quiet.

I had very good training pretending to be asleep when I was with the nuns. I think this is the only time I would ever be thankful to them.

He never stopped, he was always there come rain or shine, waiting and staring at me. What does he want? One night as I heard him get into position outside my window, I opened one eye and noticed something unusual in his hand I had not seen before. I laid there in the dark trying to make out what this shiny, silver looking thing was. I gasped in horror when I realized he was carrying his gun. As I was lying in bed I heard and visualized his every move. I knew if I ever heard him cock the gun, pulling the trigger wouldn't be far behind and that I was about to die.

CHAPTER 17

RUN HONEY! RUN!

Terror and fear are two words no child should ever have to experience in their short early life. I doubt there are any other words in the English language to describe more powerful emotions for someone so young and vulnerable to have to deal with daily. We were trapped, all of us, and there would be no end in sight for a very long time. We were living in constant dread of what would happen now in this hellish nightmare perpetrated by one man who had absolute power and control over us. Mom realised very early in her marriage to Larry that she had made another ghastly mistake. She once confided in me the only truly good thing to come out of her mistake was having her youngest son, my little brother, Ken.

She was trapped. We all were, and we had no idea how to leave or safely get away from him. Once he nonchalantly said to her while he was reading his newspaper, "Florence if you and the kids ever leave me, I can always find you and I won't be responsible for what will happen to you and the kids."

He meant it too.

It became evident throughout my years from the age of six to seventeen that I was being stealthily and cleverly manoeuvred away from my Mom. The isolating process was picking up pace as the years went by. My earliest memories of my childhood should have been happy and care-free. However, my life was now constantly in a high state of panic, stress and anxiety. The anxiety was so debilitating I developed constant stomach cramps, diarrhoea, massive migraines and insomnia that have plagued me for much of my life. With each New Year his game would change depending on his temperament, always finding new torments for me. We were the mice and he was the cat. Each new day his never-ending list of orders and edicts of things I wasn't allowed to do, things which became forbidden to have in my possession, grew ever longer. These new orders were to be obeyed without question and failure to do so would result in consequences too dreadful to comprehend.

We knew long ago that to question anything would incur a sadistic beating and the very least we could hope to endure was his endless tirade of rants and ravings. It just wasn't worth the pain of ever speaking up or asking a question. Mom and I secretly called it "Larry's law" and it was to be obeyed without question. To do otherwise was just plain stupid. From now on and for the rest of our lives my mother and I would make sure the day to day operation of the house was done to a certain standard that was laid down by him. It had to be done to his exact specifications and instructions as he dictated.

Anything different or you accidentally deviated from these instructions you simply paid the consequences.

We would try our hardest to make sure we did everything right but his orders at best were complex and confusing to follow.

In the very beginning, Larry started to make these changes shortly after they got married. Little things at first and at a glance we were not too taken aback by them as they appeared not unduly harsh or difficult to follow. But as the months slid into the years the pace began to quicken. Just as soon as the new rules were implemented and seemed to be in place, a new set of rules and regulations would be announced the very next day causing us no end of constant confusion and stress. Our towels had to be hung in a certain way with each towel hung neatly and exactly straight on the handrail and to his exact specifications. Not one should be shorter or longer than the other. As a lesson to us if this was not correctly done, someone's towel would go straight into the garbage bin and they would go without.

Another example of his crazy 'rules' was that we were not to use any more than two folds of toilet paper at any given time while in the bathroom as he stated we were using "far too much toilet paper" for his liking. He would count each perforated sheet and knew exactly how many strips were in a roll and then calculate how long that roll would last on a weekly basis per person using just the two folds. If he thought someone was using more than the required two folds, he would forbid a new roll be installed into the bathroom. We would simply have to go without until the new one was due.

In the end I got around this madness by using the school bathroom and using as much toilet paper I wanted.

Larry would then proceed to go from room to room inspecting and scrutinising our work, trying to pick something out that was wrong. You would hear his incessant mumbling as he looked at an item to see if it had been used or disturbed or touched in any way by us. I would literally tremble so badly I would often wet my pants as his inspections took place. In some far distant corner of my mind I prayed, hoping everything was to his liking but always expecting the now familiar sounds of destruction of any item that was not up to his standards. For him to destroy something was to get it out of the way and out of his sight. After his mumbling came his familiar talking to himself that everyone was touching his stuff. He would suspect one of us to have moved or touched his things. He would then scream out,

"Florence! What mother fucker touched my stuff?"

We would stop dead in our tracks and hold our breath thinking to ourselves, oh God, what's wrong now? Mom would always try covering for us, saying she touched this or that but only to clean or dust them and would apologise for not putting it back correctly in its exact spot. Sometimes she could placate him but most times it never worked. Poor Mom would accept the blame and take a quick punch to her head. To maximise what was now left of my time with Mom, I would literally run the odd mile home from school. This enabled me to spend about an hour and a half with Mom in the house before he got home at 4:30pm. I could help Mom then to make sure everything in the house met his standards of perfection. If anything was placed in a certain way by him it had to go back exactly that same way.

A pillow askew on the sofa or a knick-knack out of place would send him into an instant rage, especially if it belonged to him. He always had to have his two bath towels placed a certain way on his towel railing. His clothes were folded and arranged in in the way he determined and that was never varied. There could be no slip ups, there was no margin for errors.

And of course, the toilet rolls had to be counted.

In our short life together, Mom and I had little quality time to catch up and to talk. It seemed our precious time was now spent racing around the house making sure all was right, and everything was in its proper place for when he finally did walk through the door. If he did find something not to his likening, he would simply destroy it, no matter what it was, and out into the garbage it would go. When that dreaded hour came our fears and anxieties were palpable. We always knew of his impending arrival because the car he was driving had an unusual sound as it was backing down the driveway. This sound saved us numerous unwanted surprises. This was our signal that he was home and for us to get into our respected places. My brother and me into our bedroom and Mom on the sofa to wait for the outcome of his arrival.

Our timing and his noises were crucial to our lives.

He never did figure out that we could work out if our day or night was going to be a good or a bad one. After so many years we knew all the distinctive sounds, nuances and gestures that came out of him and we could read them accordingly.

One of many such noises that would come from him was his annoying and incessant habit of whistling then mumbling and finally talking to himself. He would have a complete conversation with himself and answer his own questions. Everything he said or did would be instantly deciphered by us as to how our day was going to go. He was that easy to read. Mom would say,

"Run honey. Run!"

I had already heard the tell-tale sound of his car and I was way on my way either running out the back door or bolting into my bedroom. Mom would then sit on the sofa clutching and wringing her hands, nervously waiting for him to come lumbering through the door to carry out his usual inspections. As she waited for him her eyes would dart about and scan the room making sure nothing was out of place. My brother would either run out the door or hide with me somewhere in our bedroom.

I would wonder, was everything perfect for him, did we do everything right, will he be happy and leave us alone? Oh God, did I forget to do this or do that? Would we get through the night? All these questions would race through our minds as we sat shaking in mortal fear. Mom tried nervously to put on a calm and cheery face in the hopes that just this once, he might be nice to us tonight. We collectively held our breath for fear that any minute he might crash through my bedroom door and drag me out by the neck to show us why we were so stupid in not doing things correctly.

Hopefully the house was the way he demanded it to be.

One day Mom and I made a fatal mistake with our allocated time together. Today the housework was done unusually early which gave us extra time up our sleeve to have a longer chat. Mom and I started talking, trying to cram as much into our short time together as possible. Previously, Larry had ordered that I was not to be seen in the presence of Mom when he was in the house. The only time for me to be with her was the half hour allocated after school. He was already making snide and ugly comments about having to feed a family of four. On this occasion, as we continued happily chatting away in the kitchen about school and your everyday mundane things in life, we forgot the time and we didn't hear the familiar sounds of his 1957 Buick as he slowly and methodically backed it down the driveway. Further we failed to notice the click of the front door opening. Mom and I were having a good time and enjoying the laughter when suddenly she gasped and turned as white as a sheet. I knew what had just happened and who was standing behind me. I turned slowly to meet his cold dead stare. I could barely whisper the words,

"I'm sorry Larry, I didn't mean to be here. It won't happen again I promise. Please don't hurt me."

As I turned to get into my bedroom and out of my window, he suddenly blocked my way with his massive arm and said,

"I thought I made myself clear to you and your Mom; you are not to be in the same room together. Who the fuck do you think you are anyway? You cock-sucking little mother-fucker."

He then lifted me up with one hand by my throat and threw me into the bedroom, slamming the door behind me. That night I got off lightly, but Mom received a terrible beating for going against his orders. I could hear her screaming and pleading,

"I'm sorry, I'm sorry, please don't hurt me daddy. I won't do it again. Please daddy don't. Please don't hurt me, please daddy, no more I beg you."

My little brother and I cowered in our room all night long as Larry rampaged through the house destroying anything he could get in his hands. The next day we woke up to the living room furniture destroyed. All that was left was the smashed remains of a coffee table, dining room table and two chairs that were now splintered pieces of wood which he threw into the fireplace to burn. The next day, everything was conveniently reduced to ashes by his ever-increasing backyard bon fires.

The never-ending stream of rules, dictates and changes kept coming, constantly catching us off our guard. It got to the point that I finally thought I was at long last going crazy because everything I did, I would stop and ask myself, 'Am I supposed to be doing it this way or does it go that way?' 'Which way is now the right way?' 'Oh God, I can't remember which way he likes it.' Then one day a new rule was announced. I was no longer allowed to watch TV at all.

Since I was now confined to my room most of time, my TV privileges I once enjoyed were now permanently denied to me. This to me was a cruel blow as TV was my only lifeline to the outside world and still held a fascination for me in those early years of the 50's & 60's. It was pure joy and a means of escape from the realities of my life.

There was never any reason given as to why he did this to me, and we certainly would never dare ask. It was just one of numerous cruel jokes, games and instructions he would deliver to me via Mom. He would never tell me personally; he would always go through Mom stating to her,

"Florence, no more fucking TV for your son. Ever! Do I make myself clear?"

"Yes daddy," she would quietly say.

For me it was a major turning point in my life as it stopped me from being near my mother or being in any room at all with her and my brother. It meant I stopped living in the real world and now lived in a world of make-believe and loneliness from the comfort of my lonely room.

One day I was desperate to watch a special program on TV that we were told would be essential for us as there would be a quiz on its contents in school the next day. Since it was a Sunday Mom said Larry would be out all day and I could "sneak a peek" if I was careful.

"Keep a sharp eye and ear out and don't let him catch you," she said to me.

We both thought it would be safe for me to quickly watch a few minutes; he certainly would be none the wiser. But unknown to us he had purposely driven around the corner, parked his car and crept back to the rear of the house to spy on us. At first, I thought I was clever in getting away with my little adventure in crime and felt relaxed enough to enjoy watching my TV program. However, he too was watching something through the kitchen window, me. My fate was sealed. He then silently slipped through the back door and crept up to stand right behind me while I was enjoying the program without a care in the world. The last thing I remember was seeing his reflection on the TV screen. I turned and gasped as he lifted me from the sofa and threw me against the wall. He ran up to the TV, spun around and spat at me saying,

"You little cocksucker! I said no TV and I mean no fucking TV. What part of that do you not understand."

I tried to tell him it was for a school project and begged him not to hurt me, promising I wouldn't do it again. As soon as I dared open my mouth, he slapped me so hard I fell onto a wooden Kench, smashing it to pieces. With that he picked up the broken pieces of wood and beat me across the head and back, yelling that he would teach me a lesson I would not soon forget. He went into a hypnotic trance while ranting incomprehensively. Just as soon as he started, he abruptly stopped in his tracks and suddenly ran out of the room and into the garage. He came back with his large axe that he always used to chop up his firewood. With one quick swing the axe came down onto the TV with an almighty crash. Anything that had the misfortune of being too close to the TV got the same treatment. As he was swinging the axe down Mom ran out the back door hoping he was not behind her with his axe. By this time, I ran into to my bedroom and jumped out the window.

He was now in his familiar mumbling, trance-like state, fixated on his destruction of the television. Nothing was going to stop him until his demons that possessed him were satisfied. Beads of sweat rolled and flicked off his face as he muttered in an incoherent voice that only he could understand. His axe finally found its mark when he struck the front of the TV screen itself. It was still turned on and it literally exploded into a ball of fire spraying him and the surrounding area with shards of glass, pieces of wood and metal. In the fifties, they still used incandescent tubes inside the TV that always reminded me of Christmas tree lights. When dropped they would always pop or explode into fine glass shards. He kept up his tirade until there was nothing left of the TV set. All over the living room lay the remains, like a butchered carcass of an animal. The flickering red lights from inside the TV could now be seen all over the carpet as they slowly faded into black. He swung around expecting me to still be there only to find I had escaped a long time ago by running off into my bedroom and jumping out the window. Larry surveyed his handiwork, but he had no idea he was now drenched in sweat and his own blood. He caught a direct hit from the exploding TV when the axe went through the picture screen and exploded directly in the face. At the time of hearing this I was hoping against hope the glass had caught him in the eyes and permanently blinded him. Maybe as a blind person he would now understand the meaning of being scared and helpless.

Wouldn't it be a nice turn of events if he was now at our mercy?

I came home later that night and was about to quietly crawl through my bedroom window to see what was left of the living room and especially the TV. Just as I was about to open my bedroom window to climb through, I suddenly gasped at the sight waiting for me as I could see the living room, and everything seemed to be destroyed.

When it was safe for Mom to re-enter the house, she called me to say the coast was clear and safe to come in. All we could do was look at the utter destruction that was now scattered everywhere. We knew what had to be done as we had done this many time before, that is, clean up the carnage as best we could. We both knew when we got back into the house hell would be waiting for the both of us. But there just wasn't anything left we could fix, mend or put back together. It was all gone. She immediately knew what must have happened and was worried for me and what we both had to face when he got home. We tried to put things back together as best we could, to make things look normal once again. It was all gone. There was less and less furniture as the years dragged by as most of the large pieces were now destroyed and replaced by cheap plastic junk. But he did leave instructions on a note for us saying,

"Clean this fucking shit up before I get back, or else."

Mom and I went into a cleaning frenzy to put back what was left of the living room and anything that was left into its rightful spot. The carpet had to be cleaned from the sprays of his blood. There was broken glass embedded in the carpet, walls and furniture. We knew it was no use, it would never look the same or be good enough for him. As the time slowly ticked by, we waited for the tell-tale sign of his car backing down the driveway. When it came Mom looked at me and we knew it was time for me to run back into my bedroom and be ready to jump out the window if need be. We no longer had to speak we just instinctively knew what we had to do.

Mom sat motionless on what was left of the couch awaiting her fate. Before I retreated, I could feel her fear and saw her hands trembling. We both knew tonight would not be a good one for any of us under Larry's roof. As his large frame lumbered in through the front door he casually glanced over to where the TV used to be. With a smirk on his face, he appeared that the mess was cleaned up to his satisfaction. It was as though he took some pride in creating all the destruction and maintaining the chronic fear in his family.

He came over to Mom who was cowering and shaking uncontrollably on the sofa expecting to get her another beating when he leaned over to her and said in a low and sinister voice

"Florence there is going to be some big changes in this house starting from right fucking now."

"Yes daddy," she wept, "Whatever you say" (he liked her calling him daddy).

He had won by his ability to remove the problem once and for all, by destroying it. We never had another TV in the house.

CHAPTER 18

THE WINDOW

It was like any ordinary window in a very ordinary bedroom. Yet this one window came to mean everything to me in my day to day survival.

Earlier, Larry had in yet another one of his many edicts, declaring that I was no longer permitted to use the front or back doors, whether he was in the house or not. There was only one window to my bedroom, and it would become my unofficial door as my only means of entry and exit. My everyday life depended now on this window for my quick escapes from whatever he had in mind for me. He had now removed the lock from my bedroom door to facilitate easier access to me. The last means of delaying his entry into my room was gone.

He ordered that my bedroom window be permanently left open regardless of the weather outside. However, one night, due to the driving rain, I quietly closed the window in the hopes he wouldn't notice. He must have heard me because as soon as I did, he came running into my bedroom screaming at the top of his voice "I said no fucking curtains, no blinds, and no closed windows."

I must have missed that memo.

In a frenzy he proceeded to rip the curtains down and with his fist began punching and smashing out the glass from the window frame, one panel at a time. Then turning his attention to the fly screens and with one kick of his foot sent them flying across the yard.

There wasn't much left of what was once a window and so to finish off his handy work he took a hammer and chisel and began breaking apart whatever might be left of it. He piled the broken glass, shredded curtains and splintered wood together in a heap and threw the remains out the window. It literally looked like a bomb had gone off with maximum damage. In the yard he poured kerosene over the entire lot and with his cigarette lighter casually lit the results of his handiwork. With a loud low boom, it went up in flames in a matter of seconds. All that was left was a large scorched patch on the lawn and a rectangular void in the bedroom wall which would be opened to the elements twenty-four hours a day, twelve months a year.

As I cowered in a corner, I stared in utter disbelief at what was once my bedroom window and looked at the destruction that was becoming part of our everyday lives again. On the plus side, Larry had given me a bigger escape route. The window he had smashed apart was now actually a bigger opening making it easier and quicker for me to jump from.

What's that old saying, "When life hands you lemons, you make lemonade."

Where would this madness take us next?

When I sat on the remains of the windowsill, the bushes outside would constantly lash my legs and chest as the rain and wind abused me while I anxiously waited for the screaming inside to either stop or escalate. This would determine if I slept inside or outside that night. I didn't mind so much the howling storm outside as it helped mask the screams coming from other parts of the house. These were the screams of my Mom being abused while objects were being smashed against the walls. This was a typical night on Barnett Way and was part of the fabric of our lives.

At times it was too much for a small child to cope with. You just couldn't get away from it. I would try to block it out by covering my ears, hiding under the bed or in the closet. Some nights I would just jump out my window with no clothes on. Later I learned to hide a pile of clothes behind an old garbage bin so I wouldn't have to roam the streets naked. I only wanted to survive another night and be left alone in peace and quiet. I had since learned to be ready for anything he might have planned for me. I was constantly on guard for anything that would cause him to come into my bedroom. Once my reaction was too slow and he grabbed me from my bed and beat me with his fists and kicking me for something I had allegedly done. Only Larry knew or cared about it in his sadistic frame of mind. It meant something to him, that's all that mattered.

I was now determined he wouldn't do that to me again. From now on I would make sure of this by sitting on the window ledge night after night, until they had apparently gone to bed and only when I thought it was safe would climb down and crawl into bed. No matter the time of year, no matter the weather, I would sit on that ledge waiting and listening.

Sitting, waiting and listening that's all I did.

Like any child all I ever wanted was to be happy and have a normal family life. My endless daydreams and fantasies while sitting on the window ledge, would transport me into the homes and lives of television families like 'Father Knows Best' or 'Leave it to Beaver.' Funny I thought, because before Larry destroyed our TV, he used to get the biggest laughs out of these sitcoms.

As I sat there, I would wonder what the neighbours must have thought when they heard the screaming coming from our house. No-one said or did anything to come and help us. No-one ever called the police, no-one ever dared question what the hell was going on next door or from across the street. Did they ever wonder or care what was happening to that poor woman and her children?

Larry made sure there would be no interference from the neighbours by intimidating them to keep them quiet. He never actually told them to keep their mouths shut, he only had to look at them a certain way and they all knew to just back away and say and do nothing. They soon realised it was healthier for them in the long run to keep quiet. Some people on Barnett Way were so terrified of Larry they even sold up and moved away.

Sometimes I would stay away for the entire night, finding it safer to sleep rough outside and as far away as possible from the house. On the occasions when Larry and Mom were 'enjoying' a drink, a funny feeling would creep over me. I knew it would always lead to them fighting as once again Larry was quick to find faults with something Mom had done. As it escalated, it was my cue to get the hell out and head to one of my safe places. I would sleep over at a friend's or find some warm and dry refuge in the backyard where I would curl up and try my best to sleep. Often, I would just roam the streets waiting for signals such as the lights going out and the screaming to subside to attempt to return through my window. I took comfort in the fact that he didn't know where I was, but I knew where he was all the time. Our game of cat and mouse continued as I strived to stay one step ahead of him and prepare myself for any eventuality.

There were times I would sit on the curb side opposite our house with absolutely no clothes on, crying my heart out while watching everything unfold through our windows like it was on a big TV screen. I knew how it would start and I always knew how it would end. He had a set plan and always managed to manoeuvre Mom straight into a trap so he would have a justifiable excuse to explode over some trivial thing either Mom or I did. He timed everything so methodically it was as if he scripted the drama himself. I would constantly try to warn Mom what he was up to, but she never listened to me. She would say I was too young to understand adults or anything about life.

Oh really?

The first thing to indicate that something was brewing was his whistling of odd tunes only he knew of. The next thing you would hear would be his crazed, unintelligible mumbling usually when drinking alcohol making it easier for him to pick a fight. After the mumbling, he would start his incessant interrogation; "Why did you do that? Who did this? When did this happen?" And so on. The smacking of his fists against his palm was the next sign that his temper was now escalating to the point where there was no chance of calming him down. It was like being sucked into a vortex from which there was no escape. Then he would suddenly explode and smash everything he could get his hands on. There was no way of ever stopping it.

If that hadn't satisfied him, he would start on us and my survival instinct kicked in. I knew what was about to happen and I got the hell out.

Unfortunately, it meant I had to abandon Mom and my young brother to fend for themselves which was agony for me. I felt then, and still do, a terrible sense of guilt that I ran out and left them to face the music. But I was so small, what was I supposed to do? What could I do? There was no one in the neighbourhood I could run to and ask for help. After banging frantically on the neighbours' front doors and pleading, "Please help me. My Mom is getting beat up, she needs help really bad." The neighbours would quickly close their doors and pretend it wasn't happening, none of them would take the chance to get involved. "No need to get involved," they would say, "It's just Flo and the kids getting beat up again."

They saw nothing and pretended not to hear anything.

Mom, by this time, had some idea of how to save herself and was always by the front door with her hand behind her back resting on the doorknob ready to make a last-minute dash for freedom. Sometimes she got away but most of the time she wasn't quick enough and would be dragged back into the house by her hair screaming for forgiveness.

There were days and nights I prayed for Larry's death, for the day when I could stand over him and watch the last breath leave his body. I wanted to hurt him so badly that I would dream of the day when I could make him suffer like he had never suffered before. I wanted him to die in a horrible and agonizing way. I wanted him to be aware that his death was imminent, and that he would be in great pain, preferably caused by me. How about poison and how would I go about administering it to him? Could I slip it into his morning coffee? Would I be able to shoot him with his gun he kept in his bedside table, or stab him to death when he was sleeping? What about poking out his eyes, rendering him helpless and totally blind? "How would you feel now Larry, helpless and living now in total darkness? How would you feel having to now depend on the three people you abused most in your life? How do you think you'll get by now Larry?"

These were the dark thoughts of a boy aged eleven.

In some twisted way, it was like watching either a drama, mystery or horror movie on TV unfolding right before our eyes. Just take your pick. It was a sad and lonely life when my world was limited to four walls, one with a massive hole through it. I jokingly told Mom that I called my room my prison-cell from hell or just 'the jail.' I would at times smile at my life and wonder where I was and where I was going to end up. Watching and listening as one storm raged on the inside while the other raged on the outside.

Numerous times I wanted to kill myself, but I was so small I had no idea how one would do something like that. There was nothing in my life worth trying to make any sense of. Around me were the reminders of Mom's never-ending screams and the continued destruction of our everyday lives.

For a Moment, all is quiet. The screams have abated. The sounds of furniture being smashed to pieces has now stopped and silence has finally settled over the house. It was my cue to sneak back through my window and into my bedroom as silently as possible. I wouldn't go straight to bed but straddle the window ledge just in case he heard me creep in and I would have to make another quick getaway. I was constantly listening for any sounds that might give him away such as the creak of the floorboards, a turn of my bedroom's squeaky doorknob or his familiar mumbling.

As always, I waited for a familiar signal from Mom such as a subtle cough, a fake sneeze or some little code words only we knew. Phrases such as "There's going to be frost on the pumpkins tomorrow" or "I think we might get some rain tonight." These would be codes for 'good night' and that all is well. Finally, the closing of her bedroom door meant Larry had preceded her into the bedroom and was now contained. It was her final signal that there would be no trouble tonight and it was safe for me to climb down from my window ledge and go to bed.

It was always after midnight when it became safe to finally slip into the warm covers of my blankets. It didn't matter if it was a school night. I still had to function the next day and act as if nothing had happened the night before. Pretending and lying became an art form for me to project that all was well in my everyday life. No one ever suspected I went to school with as little as four to five hours sleep a night. I studied either under my blankets with a torch or outside in some vacant field. Anyplace where I could find peace and quiet. I would always wear long sleeve shirts throughout the year to hide the numerous bruises on my arms. I told all my school friends my parents were very private people to ensure they would never dare visited our house.

Besides, who would want or dare to visit if they knew the truth.

Winter was the cruellest time for me. Throughout the intense winter months that window, now just a hole in the wall, stayed open to the elements regardless of the weather outside. I would still sit on the window ledge continually shivering from the intense cold. The side of my body that was dangling out in the yard would be numb from the frigid cold wind and wet from the rain. The other half of me would be in the bedroom, and partially dry. This night I felt he wouldn't be coming for me as he had got his pound of flesh from Mom the night before. Nonetheless I would still wait for hours for one of Mom's phrases or the tell-tale click of their bedroom door meaning I may get some rest tonight.

During winter the rain lashed us through the wide-open gap that once housed a window, that had once given us some protection. Now that was gone and the howling gales brought countless leaves, branches and even the odd wild animal through the window to visit us during the night. One cold night brought something new through the bedroom window, snow. A light dusting of snow now lay over our beds and floor. When I woke up, I thought, at first, my brother and I were in a scene from some winter wonderland. The fantasy was short-lived when I discovered that during the night a wild animal of some sort had crawled through the window and had eaten food I had hidden for emergencies under my bed. I kept this stash as I was never sure when I would get my next meal.

Summer had its own challenges. I dreaded this season with its stifling temperatures reaching on the average of 40-42 degrees Celsius (well over 100 degrees Fahrenheit). With the heat came the never-ending hordes of mosquitoes and flies that easily found their way straight into our bedroom. The flies owned the days and the mosquitoes ruled the nights. It was a time of misery and hardship for my brother and me. Between the constant vigils of monitoring Larry's movements and trying to avoid the flies and mosquitoes, making a meal out of me, it become almost unbearable to function in my day- to-day life.

As the seasons slowly changed and days and nights dragged on, the monotony of living like a caged animal continued. Sleep deprivation was becoming normal for me as the joys of being able to fall asleep and dream was a distant memory. A peaceful night's sleep was never going to happen because I was constantly on "guard duty" as I jokingly called it. The slightest noise or movement and my eyes would snap open, my reflexes would immediately tense up and be ready for anything. From a dead sleep I would jump out of bed and run to the window, nervously scanning my bedroom door for any sudden intrusion through it or putting my ear against the wall to hear any ominous muttering. This would happen on an average three or four times a night before I would even consider going to bed.

To this day sleep is a luxury and as elusive as ever.

I was completely cut off from my mother and everything beyond my bedroom door. I was not to be seen or heard at any time and could not move from my 'cell' while he was in the house. This forced me to sit for hours on end on the window ledge and just stare into space, not moving a muscle. My food was to be eaten in my room, if I got any. When Larry was not home Mom would give me a plate of something to eat, but it had to be eaten quickly. Often, food would secretly be put at the bottom of her laundry hamper and when the coast was clear she would haphazardly throw it quickly through my bedroom window while all the time pretending to peg her clothes out on the clothesline. At times I would be sitting on the edge of my bed when a bread and jam roll would fly past me and land on the floor. I would smile at the fact I must be the only boy in town who got his food 'airmailed' in from the backyard.

I was a total prisoner now, forbidden to ever use the bathroom toilet or to have a bath or shower. This forced me to come up with new ideas to keep myself as clean and presentable as possible for school. I would use the garden hose to wash myself, which wasn't such a problem in the summertime. In the winter, however, the hose would often be frozen solid making it impossible to keep myself clean. At these times I would sneak out late at night to the petrol station around the corner and use their water supply. Going to the toilet posed numerous problems for me but I eventually found ways of overcoming these as well. I either had to urinate out the window, (preferably when it rained so it would wash away the urine smell) or use a used bottle and store it under my bed. Night-time was my only time to be able to open my bowels and I held off until then. This was slightly more complicated as I had two options. My first option was to slip undetected out the window in the dead of night and try to find my pre-arranged hole I had dug the night before. When darkness came, I would slip out of my window and go to this hole to do my business. After I had finished, I would clean myself off with the hose and fill in the hole to burying the waste. The other option was to sneak into the petrol station around the corner and 'borrow' their toilet. After a while, Mom managed to smuggle small quantities of toilet paper to me by throwing them through the bedroom window via her nonstop airmail express.

Many a late night when the coast was clear and I was finally able to go to bed, numerous articles of school clothing, food or any other of life's necessities would come flying through my bedroom window by Mom's trusty right arm. Mom became very adept at smuggling life's little luxuries my way.

Larry of course never did find out what was going on. He prided himself on thinking he was smarter than the both of us, but we just laughed at his stupidity. It felt good to laugh, especially at his expense.

I ate, slept, and did everything else normal people took for granted either on my window ledge or out in the backyard. I had become no better than a caged animal. Larry made sure I had no friends, no family and nobody to help me. Mom and I barely communicated as our window of opportunity was now closed. We were becoming strangers to one another, almost a distant memory of what we once were, mother and son. As the years slowly moved on my despair and depression were becoming more acute. People simply gave up on me a long time ago. People had come to the door and asked for me. I wanted them to know where I was and how I lived but was at the same time felt too ashamed for them to see me living like an animal. I heard them asking questions wanting to know when I would be back. However, they were simply told by Larry that I was either out, ill or staying with relatives. Larry once even said to one of my friends that I no longer lived at this address. My isolation was now complete.

Our relatives finally gave up coming around as they either grew tired of the excuses or they knew what it was really like in our house. They would be told I was around, somewhere, but not at home now and to try calling back later. Everyone gave up on us. Then one day, I was in my room thinking I was at last alone and trying to catch up on some much-needed schoolwork when an uncomfortable and all too familiar feeling crept over me. It was a strange, overpowering sense of someone was watching me. I snapped my head around expecting to see my doorknob silently and slowly turn with Larry rushing in to grab me or him standing at my bedroom window. Long ago he worked out that the squeaky doorknob of my room alerted me to his impending entry which he remedied by oiling away my squeaky early warning system. He was now able to quietly turn the doorknob and silently open my bedroom door.

To my relief he was not standing there but for the life of me I couldn't shake off this feeling. Perhaps I was just imagining it. I started to get undressed and ready for bed when I happened to glance at a broken mirror on the wall.

He was staring at me!

I gasped when I realised where he was and what he was doing. He had been watching me through the bushes all this time and I had Momentarily let my guard down. It looked like he was back to his old tricks again. His face was distorted in the cracked mirror like he was some hideously disfigured monster. The horror of seeing him made me collapse onto my bed screaming "Please leave me alone. What do you want from me?" I shouted out to him.

It was the first time I ever angrily screamed at him and simultaneously I realized there would be dangerous consequences. I finally understood these odd, creepy feelings I had been having and that I wasn't going mad after all. He was back watching me again and this time I had ruined his fun and it was over (I thought). As I screamed, I heard him racing from the backyard and through the back door, picking up speed to get to me before I had a chance to jump out my window. I knew what I was in for by spoiling his fun and it would only be a matter of time before he would smash his way through my bedroom door. He kicked the door open with one kick so violently, breaking it off its hinges to send it flying across the room to finally land on my brother's bed. I started to jump out my window and as I was about to leap through it and out to safety, he grabbed me by my hair and slammed me to the floor. He picked me up by the throat, beat me with his fists while screaming "You cock-sucking mother fucker" and that he was going to kill me if I "ever said anything to anyone."

He dragged me down the hallway and threw me into their bedroom. I landed very close to his bedside table where he kept his gun. Thoughts of grabbing the gun and killing him filled my head. I inched closer to the side table as he blocked any escape, leaving me trapped in their bedroom thinking 'Well this is either fight or die.' Just then Mom hurried in and jumped between Larry and me. It was as if she knew what I was planning to do. She stopped me just in time as I was inches away from grabbing his gun and killing him then and there. By distracting Larry, she gave me time to get out of their room. I ran straight to my bedroom and dived into the backyard from window.

It would have been so much easier for all of us if I had managed to use the gun. Little did I know Mom had come closer than I did in trying to kill him on a previous occasion. A few months earlier, in the dead of the night when Larry was sleeping off his Highballs (whisky and water) she got his gun, cocked it and pulled the trigger only to realize the gun didn't fire due to the safety catch being on. After fumbling with the safety catch and finally releasing it, Mom lowered the gun towards his head and took aim straight at his temple but hesitated Momentarily to suddenly realise if she shot him who's going to look after her kids? She quietly returned it to his drawer as she had found it. She said to me later "I just couldn't shoot the bastard because if I did, they would put me in prison and take you kids away, and I wouldn't be allowed to see my boys ever again." Larry never knew how close he came to death not once but twice.

Once again, I was saved by my mother and that bedroom window.

CHAPTER 19

HAPPY BIRTHDAY SON

From six to seventeen years of age happiness was rarely a part of my life thanks to Larry, but I never stopped hoping for it. In my eyes a happy family was a total myth perpetuated by Hollywood Sitcoms of the 50's and 60's. Perched on that damn window ledge, I would daydream constantly and ask myself what would it be like to be free of worry, stress and never having to look evil in the eye again? That evil that was always only a few feet from me. As the years rolled by, I would dream for my eighteenth birthday to come so I could get as far away from this hell as fast as humanly possible.

My seventeenth birthday was approaching so that time of escape was not far away. About this time Mom came home from work to hear the familiar sounds of screams as she ran to my bedroom to see Larry kicking me repeatedly in the head. She tried to pull him off and I could remember her saying "Please daddy stop, no more, you're going to kill him!"

My concern was for her to get away as I knew if she got involved, he would turn and lash out at her. Unfortunately for Mom he swung around and with a single, massive punch, knocked Mom unconscious. She woke up the next day with many of her teeth either broken or knocked out of her mouth, but she never went to a doctor for help. She was still expected to get up like nothing out of the ordinary happened the night before, cook his usual breakfast of two eggs, over easy, bacon and toast. The table was still set to meet his standards and his food cooked to his exact specifications - eggs runny, crispy bacon and the toast hot. Mom was barely able to see out of her swollen and badly blackened eyes, much less stand and cook a meal for him. I remember thinking to myself that I couldn't believe this was our Mom who now looked so tiny hunched over a stove trying to cook. She shook with fear, hoping to get his breakfast done correctly. As he began to eat, she held her breath. Was everything alright? All Mom heard coming from him were his usual grunts.

This beating was on another level. Usually Larry was careful not to leave any tell-tale marks that could be plainly seen. If there was no visible bruising, then there would be no need for an explanation should anyone ask about them. This time he was careless, and it was going to be difficult for me to explain away the clearly apparent injuries to the people around me. Besides, I just didn't care any longer what I looked like or who saw it.

By this time, we had reached rock bottom. I wanted the world to see what kind of a monster he was. Friends and family will soon know what's going on. I was no longer ashamed. There would be no more excuses. There would be no more hiding, and he was going to pay.

My teenage years had gone from bad to worse when my health took an unexpected turn. I had to be hospitalized for various problems, my neck and back were permanently damaged, and I suffered severe headaches, no doubt from the numerous head fractures and beatings Larry gave me. It was almost my seventeenth birthday and as birthdays go it was just another day which was never celebrated. Gone were the days of youthful expectations of birthday presents. In fact, I never told anyone at school what day it was.

What would I have to celebrate anyway?

As I was running home from school one day, I noticed a pall of smoke coming from the general direction of our house. At first, I thought someone was burning off autumn leaves as that's what everybody in the neighbourhood did. As I got closer to my house I suddenly slowed down from my usual run to a slow walk. Nearer still, and I could see Larry's car unexpectedly parked in the driveway. He had come home early that day for some unknown reason. As I got closer to get a better look, my heart was pounding so I managed to hide in our next-door neighbour's bushes to see Larry quickly emerge from the backyard, get into his car and speed away. Whatever he was up to he was burning something in the backyard, and it was now well and truly an inferno. He obviously wanted to leave before I got home. When he was finally out of sight I crept slowly into the backyard and I was shocked by what I saw. He had taken all my clothes, shoes and personal belongings from my bedroom, poured petrol over them, burning the entire lot in one gigantic bonfire. I tried desperately to rescue something, anything from the fire, which was now raging out of control, but it was too late. There was nothing left to save. I had only the ashes that were once my belongings to poke through. There was nothing left. All traces of me even being on this planet were all gone.

This was another example of his many attempts to erase me once and for all from our house on Barnett Way.

Just then Mom came home from work and came around to the back of the house to see what was going on. As she got closer to the fire she gasped in disbelief. We both shook our heads quietly sobbing, amazed at the trouble he would go through just to get rid of me.

As we stood there trying to make sense of everything, Mom found a Birthday card by the fire that said, 'Happy Birthday Son' and signed 'Daddy'. I crumpled into a heap of tears. I just couldn't take any more and wondered what his next move would be. As I was still considered a minor by law, he legally couldn't kick me out of the house until I was eighteen years old. I had to endure this for another year? Could Mom and I wait that long?

It then dawned on me and I turned to Mom and said, "I'm so sorry Mom but I have to go and go now! It's that or be taken away either in an ambulance or a body bag." There was no choice. As difficult as it was for Mom and me, we both knew it was time for me to leave quickly before it was too late. She nodded reluctantly in agreement as the tears fell slowly down her cheeks.

Then one day I was talking to a workmate at McDonalds. As luck would have it, he was looking for someone to share an apartment with him and I jumped at the offer. I moved that day into his apartment which was several blocks from our house. Far enough away from Larry but still close enough for Mom to see me. My share of the rent would be $30 a month and since I was now working after school at McDonalds, I could just afford it. For the first time in my life I started to feel safe and not worry about what waited for me behind closed doors. I thought at long last I would sleep peacefully and be free from the fear of being attacked at any given Moment. I had a TV that worked and a bedroom window that closed.

By now I was focused on one thing and one thing only, what would Larry do to Mom or my brother, now that I was no longer his punching bag? Would he use Mom even more as one or would he now start on a fresh new project, my little brother? However, my new-found freedom and happiness quickly evaporated.

One day phone calls mysteriously started at all hours of the day and night. At first there was an unusual clicking noise on the other end, followed by heavy breathing. It was Larry! He had found me! I just knew it was him and all my old terrors came racing back to me. There was no place to run, no place to hide. What do I do now? Where do I go? I slumped down into a corner of my room and sobbed uncontrollably.

Different room same cage.

The phone calls continued. My roommate even had to change our number, not once, but three times. It would seem Larry always found a way to find it. Then we began taking the phone off the hook at night but something new was added to my torment. When we both had gone to bed about an hour or two would go by when someone would violently bang on our front door and by the time, we looked out through the peep hole, they were mysteriously gone. This went on for months. Most nights when alone I would just cower in my corner of my room, cover my ears and wait for his torment to hopefully end. Police were called but unless we had proof that it was Larry, they couldn't help.

Again, I felt powerless, alone and afraid.

My days were filled with the constant banging on my door and the never-ending mysterious phone calls. I was so exhausted from lack of sleep. The creepy feeling that I was being watched and followed all the time never left me. I was eventually asked to move out from my friend's apartment, after only being there for a year, because he found it too stressful.

He doesn't know what stress is.

Soon I found myself living on a nightly basis on different friend's sofas. By now I was always on the move, constantly looking over my shoulder, which seemed to keep me on a never-ending treadmill of trying to find a safe place to sleep, work, and go to school. Anything to keep one step ahead of Larry.

CHAPTER 20

ESCAPE TO OZ

October 1969

It will soon be my nineteenth birthday and I'm in college. I have been here for several months. It's difficult for me because I don't enjoy it as it's impossible for me to concentrate on my studies. My grades were falling, and I had lost interest in everything, including school and life. It would be only a matter of time before I would fail college and eventually leave.

One day as I was sitting in a lecture, vaguely listening to a visiting college professor when he suddenly went off his subject and started talking about Australia needing immigrants to come work and settle. This was my epiphany to end all epiphanies and I wasted no time applying at the Australian Consul in San Francisco.

I think I'm going to Australia!

The weeks dragged by when at last I received an important looking envelope in the mail with the Australian coat of arms impressively stamped on the front. To my delight they had finally granted me permission to go and make a new life in Australia. I had saved $600 from my job at McDonalds that was just enough to buy a one-way ticket (which was $530.50) but not nearly enough to live on once there. But who cared? I could always find a job. I hurriedly bought my ticket to freedom to a country called Australia. Nothing could possibly be as bad as my living conditions were now, so I happily handed over my hard-earned money to an airline called Qantas.

By the way, where is Australia? And what's a Qantas?

That night some friends of mine took me out for a few drinks to celebrate my eventual escape. We all got very drunk, but I had sense enough not to get in their car to get home. I told them I'm just down the road and will be fine to get home on my own. The last thing I needed was to get stopped by the police or worse still get into a car accident. I wasn't about to let anything happen to me that might jeopardise my plans.

I waved them off and staggered down the road towards my place.

I had walked about a half mile when suddenly a carload of men pulled onto the sidewalk, cutting off my path. Some of the men jumped out of the car, grabbed me and pulled something over my head. They opened the door and threw me, screaming, into the back seat. I could hear some guys in the front seat talking and laughing saying this will get them the needed points for their Fraternity nominations. I guessed by the different sounds of their voices there was at least three of them up front. I could feel there were another two in the backseat, one on each side of me. We seemed to drive for miles, and I had no idea where we were going or what was going to happen to me.

Death seemed the only way out for me.

We finally came to a sudden and unexpected halt. The back door opened and several of them dragged me kicking and screaming out into a vacant field where they proceeded to take turns beating and raping me for what seemed like several hours. After they had their 'fun' I was bundled back into the car and eventually thrown out of it down a lonely back road while it was still moving. I staggered to my feet bleeding but determined to find my way home no matter how long it might take. I no longer had my shoes and had barely enough clothes on me to get home without anyone looking at me suspiciously or attracting attention from the police. I certainly didn't need any police. I did not want anything to jeopardise my plans for Australia. No questions. No delays.

I was still determined to leave for Australia on the time and date allocated to me by the Consul. I wanted to go after my nineteenth birthday so I could arrive before Christmas 1969.

During the days and weeks after the rape I suddenly developed blinding headaches, fevers and nonstop bleeding from my rectum. My impending departure date was coming up and nothing, but nothing was going to stop me from boarding that Qantas flight. I seemed to rally, and the headaches and fevers subsided but I kept bleeding on and off for a very long time. I was to leave on a Friday afternoon and Mom had pre-warned me that Larry somehow found out what I was about to do and went on one of his most violent rampages to date. Sometime during the night Mom managed to slip a note under my door to warn me he knew everything and was going to be at the airport to do any and everything he could to prevent me from leaving.

Why I thought? Am I that much of a threat to him?

Now my paranoia was in overdrive. Did he have something to do with my kidnap and rape? I just couldn't think straight and pushed that to the back of my mind as desperation set in. I had to think fast as he was quickly closing in on me. He had known all along my plans for escape. But how? In a blind and panic-stricken state of mind, I stuffed whatever I could grab into my small suitcase. Whatever I touched that was mine, in it went. Speed was paramount for me to make a clean get away.

I begged the airline to change my departure flight and arranged to leave a day earlier. But I was so torn to leave my poor Mom and little brother behind. I felt I was betraying them and leaving them to the mercy of that man. We both knew what she was in for once I was safely out of the picture. It would be only a matter of time before he started doing to my brother what he did to me. She would only say "Go, get away from here and be happy for once in your life! Stop worrying about us!"

The day finally arrived for my planned escape. Would he find out? Would he be waiting for me? He knew I was planning this trip to Australia, but did he know I had changed the dates of my departure? I got into the back seat of taxicab and hid low down in the seat as we drove to the small airport that serviced our town in the final hours of daylight. This was my first ever trip on an airplane and wondered what I was getting myself into.

There would be no turning back. Escape was now or never.

The airport consisted of just one runway and back in 1969 there was no such thing as security like there is now. People could get as close to the airplane as possible providing they stood behind a small cyclone fence. Passengers only could progress beyond the small fence. Hugs were exchanged over the fence before they would board their plane. I had no one to hug or say goodbye so I hid in the airport toilet until the very last call was made to board the plane. I hurriedly boarded the small propeller driven aircraft that would take me as far as San Francisco. I quickly found my window seat. I'm not sure if I was more nervous of flying for the first time or of Larry finding me. My head was darting from left to right, forward and aft of the plane expecting to see him sitting in a seat not far from me, staring at me with his all too familiar grin.

Would he be the last to come on? For god sake let's go. Hurry up! What's taking so long? I screamed over in my head.

The longer we stayed on the ground the more agitated I became. At long last the door finally closed, and we started to do a slow push back from our gate. As I settled back, trying to relax for what would be my next big adventure, I glanced out my window and gasped in utter horror and disbelief at what was staring back at me. Larry was standing at the fence glaring straight at me. He had just missed me by minutes.

But how? How did he find out the day I was leaving? I discovered later that he forced the information from Mom by severely beating her. The poor thing finally cracked and just couldn't take anymore, and I certainly never blamed her. Now I could see him running back and forth along the fence like some demented caged animal, screaming and hurling abuse at either me, the pilot or at the plane itself. Shouting, spitting and screaming as he tried frantically to have my plane stopped. I could see the foam forming at the sides of his mouth he was in such a rage of disbelief that I had at long last tricked him and got away with it.

How does it feel Larry, now that you're no longer in control?

He was in a total rage, shaking and pulling back and forth on the fence as if he was trying to pull it down like you see some Gorillas do when in a zoo cage. As I was watching him, I could just hear him over the noise of the propellers screaming out his foul obscenities. The plane slowly taxied by him. Finally, after several agonizing minutes, the Captain came over the PA system to say we are now about to line up to the active runway for an on-time departure to San Francisco. As the plane slowly went by him, he was still screaming his filthy tirades. I slowly turned to face him from my window seat making sure he could get a real good look at me as we slowly taxied by. When he spotted me, I beamed a defiant smile, casually held up both my hands and extended my two middle fingers while silently mouthing the words

"Fuck you Larry!"

At last I thought, I had finally won and beaten him. I win, you lose. Oh, there wasn't a better feeling! I then made an over-the-top gesture of happily waving goodbye to him with a handkerchief like I really was going to miss him and pretending to shed tears. I finally got to San Francisco and boarded my Qantas 707 jet. As I settled back into my seat, I smiled smugly to myself, now I know what a Qantas is. The flight was longer than I expected, stopping at places I had never heard of or been to before such as romantic Hawaii, exotic Fiji and finally exciting Sydney. I arrived in Sydney, Australia with less than $60. U.S in my pocket, but I didn't care. It was December 11, 1969.

I was out of my cage, safe and free. For the first time in my life I felt alive and could now walk around the streets knowing he's finally nowhere near me.

My only sadness was that I left in such a panic I never got to say goodbye to my Mom, brother, family and friends. I wanted to thank Mom for all the sacrifices she made for me over the years and maybe try to warn my brother what might be waiting for him.

CHAPTER 21

POST-MORTEM 2018

December 11, 1969

I safely arrived into Australia and one month into my nineteenth birthday.

As soon as my feet touched this wonderful country, I literally fell in love with it and have not stopped living life since. It was summer and for once I could feel free walking along the beaches soaking up the fresh air, the sunshine and not ever having to look over my shoulder. I had packed in such a blind panic all I found inside my bag when I unpacked was as a pair of underwear, one shoe and a heavy coat. I had no idea then about the seasons being back-to-front. I never laughed so hard and for such a long time in my entire life.

It felt great.

It was hard the first few years living in a new country when everything you knew from your previous life was completely different. I now set goals to make a better life for myself something I could only dream about in my previous life. I worked hard sometimes in dead end jobs and saved like crazy. As time went by, I finally had some money in the bank I could call my own, a roof over my head that didn't belong to someone else and my own bed to sleep in. Couch surfing or finding a warm spot in someone's back yard was now a thing of the past.

And yes, I had the biggest and best T.V you could buy. I can watch what I want, when I want and for once without fear.

Unfortunately, Larry did find a way to follow me to Australia. I naively thought I had left him behind, and all the evil memories associated with him were now well and truly in the past. Larry was back and just as malignant and full of vengeance to torment me in the present. He would now come back to me exclusively to plague me throughout the night.

My brother and I have always suffered from sleep deprivation or some type of insomnia. I can honestly say five hours of fitful sleep a night would be a good night for me. If I was fortunate to have those five hours of sleep, it would be punctuated by horrific nightmares filled with hellish screams coming from Larry. He was back in my mind in to get his pound of flesh out of me. On some nights I would wake up screaming like a banshee thinking I was back in the house on Barnett Way. I would jump out of bed in a blind panic and run helter-skelter towards what I thought was my old escape window. Instead of leaping out this window, I would ultimately slam myself into a solid brick wall and wake myself up dazed and confused on the floor.

I needed help to exorcise Larry once and for all.

The best part of my new life was never having to look over my shoulder. Windows and doors were now a normal part of my life – no longer escape routes.

My mother however, had one too many beatings over the ensuing years and eventually had reached the end of her tether. Thanks to my brother, who came to her rescue, she recovered and found, for the second time in her life, the courage to finally leave a brutal man and eventually divorce him. She was so anxious to put an end to her miserable marriage she signed literally everything over to him, asking for and receiving nothing. What she did leave behind was either ruined or destroyed anyway, but she didn't care because she finally had happiness and was free from Larry.

My brother came through when I could not.

A few years later, out of the blue, Larry called Mom and begged her to come back to him so she could look after him as he was diagnosed with pancreatic cancer and was given two weeks, at best, to live. Mom being always the kind and caring soul she was, took pity on him and considered going back to nurse him until he passed away. It was after all only for a couple of weeks.

She had forgiven him a long time ago.

My brother Kenny had the sense to see through his charade and at the last minute put a stop to her going. He knew if she went back to look after him, he would kill her in revenge for daring to leave him. If he couldn't have her alive, he would make damn sure she preceded him into death. Mom always struggled with the word 'no' as no was not in her vocabulary. For the first time in her life she was brave enough to finally say the actual word "no" to Larry and that she would not be able to look after him.

I received a phone call from Mom a couple weeks later to say, "Larry just killed himself." After a stunned silence I asked Mom how she felt. Mom said she was at peace now and hoped he was too.

Larry killed himself the previous evening by putting the gun he always had in his bedside table into his mouth, blowing his brains out. The sad thing about it all was I think everyone sighed with relief on hearing the news of his death. I hope my brother found some peace as well in his passing. There was one bullet still lodged in the gun chamber. Deep down we all knew that the remaining bullet was meant for Mom.

In 1990 Mom was diagnosed with early onset dementia. Doctors said it was not surprising considering the constant beatings she endured whilst with Larry. As I could not always be there, I am forever grateful to my brother for the constant care and love he gave Mom and for being by her side as she passed.

I continue to live in God's Own Country, Australia. This country that saved me and gave me a second chance at life, love and happiness with my long-suffering partner of the last thirty-four years, Tony, who has patiently helped me write this story.

Since Larry died, I have not had a single night terror.

I may have been born on November 14, 1950 in the United States but for me I was reborn on my arrival into Sydney, Australia, December 11, 1969.

Life is good at 68. And it is great to be free.

Your outlook on life will determine your path in life.

The end

ABOUT THE AUTHOR

After permanently leaving the United States in December,1969 at 19 years of age, Greg Lloyd-Wadsworth migrated to Australia, becoming a citizen.

He previously lived in Sydney for over 40 years.

He has worked in various industries of hospitality, banking, domestic airlines reservations and 32 years for Qantas Airlines of Australia from 1974-2006 in the role of a flight attendant, on board manager, cabin crew interviewer and facilitator.

He has since retired where he and his partner of 34 years have moved to Queensland, Australia where they spend much of their time travelling.

www.ingramcontent.com/pod-product-compliance
Lightning Source LLC
LaVergne TN
LVHW091303080426
835510LV00007B/368